SPARTAN
FIT!

SPARTAN
FIT!

30 DAYS.
TRANSFORM YOUR MIND.
TRANSFORM YOUR BODY.
COMMIT TO GRIT.

Joe De Sena

with John Durant

HOUGHTON MIFFLIN HARCOURT
BOSTON   NEW YORK   2016

Copyright © 2016 by Joe De Sena and Spartan Race, Inc.

For information about permission to reproduce selections from this book, write to trade.permissions@hmhco.com or to Permissions, Houghton Mifflin Harcourt Publishing Company, 3 Park Avenue, 19th Floor, New York, New York 10016.

www.hmhco.com

Library of Congress Cataloging-in-Publication Data is available.
ISBN 978-0-544-43960-3

Printed in the United States of America
DOC 10 9 8 7 6 5 4 3 2
4500615391

Dictionary entries "spartan" and "Spartan" are adapted and reproduced by permission from *The American Heritage Dictionary of the English Language, Fifth Edition.* Copyright © 2011 by Houghton Mifflin Harcourt Publishing Company.

To ancient Spartans,
for modern Spartans

CONTENTS

spar·tan *adj.*

1. Rigorously self-disciplined.
2. Simple, frugal, or austere.
3. Marked by brevity of speech; laconic.
4. Courageous in the face of pain, danger, or adversity.

Spar·tan *n.*

1. A citizen of Sparta.
2. One of Spartan character.
3. One who has completed a Spartan Race.

PROLOGUE:
BLINDFOLDED AND BOUND

JAY JACKSON WAS BLINDFOLDED. His hands were tied behind his back, his feet lashed together. A washcloth was shoved down his throat, a pillowcase cinched around his mouth to keep the gag in place. And a gun was pointed at his head.

An hour and a half earlier Jay had been drifting to sleep in his bed — until a man opened his bedroom door, flipped on the light, and pulled out a gun.

"Roll over," the man ordered.

"What are you doing?"

"ROLL. OVER."

The man tied up Jay's hands and feet with thin satin ropes he pulled from his pockets, plus shoelaces, neckties, and dress shirts taken from Jay's closet. Then he blindfolded him. The gag would come later — after more than an hour of bizarre conversation covering everything from mundane details of Jay's life (details that the man already knew) to a high-stakes interrogation of whether Jay might be able to identify him to the police. It became disturbingly clear that the man hadn't come for money and he wasn't in a hurry to leave.

Then, the gag.

Then it was quiet.

It's hard to overstate the feelings of disorientation and anxiety from being unable to see. Humans are visual animals; we depend on sight more than any other sense to navigate the world. Everyone has stumbled to the bathroom in pitch blackness — it's hard to gauge distance, direction, and body position; it's easy to stub a toe, trip, and fall. The simplest movement becomes a complex maneuver.

Being blindfolded makes one thing easier: seeing your life flash before your eyes.

Jay thought back to his childhood when his father would make him and his older brother wrestle on the mat in their basement — while blindfolded. Using only touch, muscle memory, and the mind's eye, they maneuvered for an advantage with a disadvantage, trying to pin the other to the floor.

Wrestling blindfolded was their father's crazy idea.

"If you practice in tougher conditions, the match will seem easy," he said.

Then he reminded them (for what seemed like the thousandth time) about Doug Blubaugh, 1960 Olympic gold medalist in wrestling, whose eyesight was so bad that he was said to be legally blind when he took off his Coke-bottle glasses before every match.

"Learn to anticipate your opponent even when you can't see him," their father coached.

Easier said than done. Jay's brother got position, hooked Jay's arm, flipped him on his back, and pinned him. Jay would eventually develop into the better wrestler, but at that point his older brother was stronger and more experienced.

"Fight back," their father encouraged. "Keep fighting back."

Their father made them practice until exhaustion (or until their mother interceded). But that's what happens when your dad is also the high school gym teacher: weekend wrestling practice in the basement, occasionally blindfolded.

All the other kids at school thought Jay's dad was way too

intense — a stern, no-excuses, work-your-ass-off, actions-speak-louder-than-words type of guy. He emphasized hard work but didn't really enforce it with *external* discipline — Jay was never grounded, for example — so much as he encouraged and cultivated *internal* discipline. He was also a Green Beret, a fact that didn't really surprise Jay — except that he didn't learn it until the eighth grade, when a classmate told him. Jay went home and asked his dad if it was true. "Yeah," he said with characteristic nonchalance. A Green Beret didn't need to tell anyone.

Disciplined, tough, laconic, modest — that was Paul Jackson. And maybe a little crazy, especially in a safe, soft, affluent suburban world where his strict discipline seemed antiquated at best, punitive at worst. A man fit for tougher times. A man who taught his children to view every obstacle as an opportunity. A man crazy enough to train his sons to wrestle blindfolded.

But right now, none of that training would matter if Jay couldn't get his hands free — they were still tied up with shirts, ties, shoelaces, and ropes. His feet were tied too, he was gagged and blindfolded, and there was a man with a gun in the room. It would be an escape that Houdini never made.

Jay knew he could die. But rather than panic or give up, he heard his father's voice. He chose to make this a challenge, just another obstacle to overcome. Almost a game.

Quietly and imperceptibly, Jay was able to loosen the shirts and ties — thicker and easier to undo than the shoelaces and ropes — but he had to stop short, because his hands were exposed to view and he couldn't just break them apart.

Jay needed a way to cover his hands. So he pretended to shiver. To Jay's astonishment, the man took the bait and put a blanket over him — covering Jay's hands from sight. Then the man suggested turning off the bedroom light. Most people would have been terrified — was the man about to pull the trigger? But Jay, thinking back to wrestling blindfolded as a kid, knew it would give him an advantage. He emphatically nodded. Now, not only were his hands out of sight, but his captor was also in the dark.

Then, in a terrifying act of intimacy, the man lay down on the bed next to Jay. Jay could hear him breathing.

But Jay stayed focused on the next step: untying his hands. The next step was all that mattered. Every little bit was a little bit closer to survival. Thankfully, while being tied up he had the instinct and presence of mind to force his hands slightly apart, which left a little space between his right and left palms — room to wriggle. If his hands had been flush, he never would have been able to free them.

Jay had learned this maneuver from the unlikeliest of places: college hazing. He had been the only freshman on the varsity wrestling team, and the upperclassmen got a laugh out of tying him up and tossing him on the pool table. Never in a million years did Jay imagine that one day he might have to thank them for doing that. But it made him stronger.

It took six or seven minutes to free his hands. Then Jay slowly, quietly brought his hands in front of him. He would probably have only one chance to grab the man, restrain him, and take away the gun. But Jay's feet were still tied, he was still gagged and blindfolded, and he couldn't see exactly where the man was. But he could still *hear* where he was.

So Jay mumbled something.

"What?" the man said, inadvertently giving away his approximate location.

Jay mumbled again.

"What'd you say?" the man asked.

That was enough to pinpoint his location. Jay lunged at him with his now-free hands, grabbing and wrapping the man's torso, then moving directly to his wrists. Shocked, the man growled that

he had a gun, but Jay could feel the man's wrists and empty hands
— he was bluffing. Had the gun dropped?

Thank God I was a wrestler and not a tennis player.

After Jay had the man's wrists, he jammed the man's head between the bed and a chair, wrestled him off the bed, took the upper
position, and pinned his back to the ground. Then Jay managed to
take off the blindfold and gag. But there was no way to untie his feet
while restraining the man. And the man was struggling, using his
feet to push the bindings around Jay's feet. His ankles burned and
bled, but Jay ignored the pain. If the man stood up, it was all over.

Jay would have to knock him out — but he had never been in a
real fight before. So he started to headbutt the man, over and over
and over, until their faces were covered in blood.

For the next fifteen minutes, they wrestled on the floor. (A
college wrestling match lasts a total of seven minutes.) They had
moved around the foot of the bed to the other side, where the man
grabbed a telephone cord — which Jay then grabbed, looped around
the man's neck, and pulled tight with his right hand while using his
elbow to pin down the man's arm. With his left hand, Jay picked up
the phone and dialed 911.

At first the officers didn't seem to believe it. It was about 4 a.m.
and this stuff rarely happens in Palo Alto. The police arrived at the
front door five minutes later.

The dispatcher on the phone asked Jay to go answer the door.

Jay was, of course, a little tied up at the moment.

"Tell them to break down the door!"

Then, to the disbelief of anyone fighting off an intruder with
their bare hands, the dispatcher said that the police couldn't break
down the door. It would require a supervisor's approval. That took
another twenty minutes. That meant Jay's life depended on pinning
down a grown man — while Jay's legs were tied up and a gun was

perhaps within reach — for more than thirty-five minutes. Finally the police arrived, guns drawn, and it was over.

For Jay, his new life had just begun. He picked up the phone, called his dad, and thanked him. Later he learned that he had become a cult hero to the paramedics. They had never seen anyone beaten up as badly as the intruder by just one person.

The wrestling match of Jay's life didn't take place on the mat. There were no rules of engagement, no referee with a whistle, no timer, and no water breaks. The conditions were unpredictable and unfair, and they changed on the fly. And as Jay (and eventually his opponent) learned, there is a massive difference between a practice fight and the fight of your life.

Prepared for anything life throws at you — that's Spartan Fit.

1

GET TO THE STARTING LINE

"The bravest are surely those who have the clearest vision of what is before them, glory and danger alike, and yet notwithstanding, go out to meet it."

— THUCYDIDES

MY NAME IS Joe De Sena, and if all you want is a training program, there's a list of exercises in chapter 6 and recipes starting on page 206.

Or, to make things *really* simple: Go outside right now and run as far as you can. Then do as many burpees as you can. Then run, walk, or crawl home. Eat whole foods, skip dessert, don't get drunk, get some sunshine, take cold showers, lift something heavy, use the stairs, meditate or pray, find someone to love. Lights out at 8 p.m.

There's your program — go do it.

Look, if being fit were as easy as having a list of the right exercises, the Internet would have ended the obesity crisis. There are a gazillion exercise programs out there! The team at Spartan Race posts a new workout every day — it's all there, it's all free. We have all this information at our fingertips. Lack of information isn't your main obstacle.

Your main obstacle is *you*.

You are also your greatest opportunity.

And that's as true for me as it is for anyone.

The purpose of this book is to help you overcome any physical or mental obstacle — and to achieve the opportunity that lives inside of you. To become Spartan Fit.

Specifically, this book contains a 30-day training program to prepare you to complete a Spartan Race, an obstacle race that I founded and oversee. Spartan Race drives competitors to their limits so they can surpass them. Our tagline is "You'll know at the finish line"—and you will—but I spend much of my time imploring people around the world to get to the starting line, which is even tougher. Once they're there, the race takes over.

As tough as it is to get some people to the starting line, I'm constantly amazed by what those same people accomplish *after* the finish line. Jay Jackson didn't wrestle blindfolded because he thought it might save his life one day; he trained for a sport and it changed his life in a way that he never could have anticipated. After that experience, Jay changed his career, became a high school teacher, and developed a curriculum with us called Spartan Edge to help kids overcome any obstacle through grit and toughness. I've received tens of thousands of emails from disabled veterans, cancer survivors, and ordinary folks who went on to do extraordinary things beyond the finish line. I'm committed to helping others build more strength and grit to achieve their goals in sports *and* life. I love to inspire people to achieve the seemingly impossible.

I'm an ultraendurance athlete who has been lucky enough to compete in challenging races all over the world. I have completed more than fifty ultramarathons, and more Ironman events than I remember. Most of these races were one hundred miles or more, with a few traditional marathons mixed in. I was roped into competing in the Vermont 100, the Lake Placid Ironman, and the Badwater Ultra in one week. The last of those events is a 135-mile run that travels from Death Valley to Mount Whitney in the middle of summer. That year it was 137 degrees. My shirt melted.

Yet, no matter the challenge, I never question whether I'll finish a race. The rush of the starting gun drops me into an empty space where I hear nothing but the sound of my own breathing and the drumbeat of my heart. My body moves forward, but everything else stands still. I'm not thinking about hopes or regrets, what I'm having for dinner, or what my kids are doing. All I'm thinking about, if it's thinking at all, is the repetitive *thwap* of my feet striking the pavement. I will finish, no matter how far I must go to reach the finish line. It's simply what must happen.

As for why I'm so compelled to compete, I think back to my childhood in Queens, New York, in the 1970s. My mother introduced me to yoga, an ancient form of holistic training that captivated her imagination and changed her life, bringing calm to her troubled mind. True yoga masters could hold a pose for minutes, hours, or days. It wouldn't make much difference, because for them time stopped. They had mastered the relationship between their mind and body to such a degree, fused them so completely, that nothing mattered other than the sound of their breath and the beating of their heart.

But even if you practice yoga, meditate, or run for hours on end, life will intrude in ways that leave you unprepared. Obstacles confront you and require quick adaptations, making a mockery of something like "the runner's high." So you're cruising along, feeling in control of the situation? Great. How about when the trail ends and the terrain grows rocky and you break your ankle? Then what do you do? Or what happens when you need to climb a rock face to keep advancing — only, come to think of it, you didn't train for that, and you could easily fall and break your neck? Do you adapt, or do you fall apart, because all you knew was the thud of the pavement, and now the pavement is gone?

Forget the challenges of an endurance run — some people are so ill-equipped at handling the unexpected that a cold cup of coffee or a traffic jam can ruin their day. Very seldom do we wake up and have our day unfold exactly as mapped, so I grew interested in how physically unprepared many people are for daily events, let alone extraordinary ones. Their training doesn't reflect life's complexities. An event such as a distance race, as challenging as many people find it to be, is highly predictable — an adjective that seldom applies to life's great challenges, the ones that truly define us as human beings. If a 5K race seems like a good impetus for improving your health, consider an alternative, one that's not totally preplanned and that will strengthen your mind as well as your body. Consider a Spartan Race.

I created the Spartan Race in 2010 to test people's overall conditioning, a term that encompasses endurance, strength, stamina, speed, and athleticism. I also wanted to test their ability to adapt physically — and, perhaps even more importantly, *mentally* — especially to surprises. I wanted to stress test the weaknesses that make us vulnerable in a difficult and sometimes dangerous world, where the chaos of the battlefield increasingly characterizes civilian life and everyday society. My theory was that such a test would have broader implications for a person's life than mere fitness. Attempting a Spartan Race, I believed, would teach people to handle the obstacles of everyday life, enabling them to function at a high level as parents, employees, public servants, or in any role that life might throw their way.

Spartans refer to this readiness as "obstacle immunity," meaning an ability to move past, around, through, or over what life places in their path. In the races, we'll position a mud pit, a greased wall, and other physical challenges in the way of racers — but, whatever the obstacle, its purpose goes beyond just trying to trip someone up and challenge them with thirty burpees. These obstacles are metaphors for the obstacles we all encounter as we move through life. A cancer diagnosis is an obstacle. A pink slip is an obstacle. A broken marriage is an obstacle. Life sends them our way in an endless procession.

Spartan Race was conceived as a test, but no one should race

—at least not like this—without adequate training. The absence of physical conditioning would lead to failure, plain and simple. In my mind, the *training* for the race, even more than the race itself, was where the major life progress would occur.

An athlete training for a Spartan Race poses the same challenges as a jazz musician preparing to give a performance. It requires extensive preparation, but its content can't necessarily be predicted. Musicians can't prepare for the concert by rehearsing what they know they'll play; it wouldn't be jazz without improvisation. What they have to do is train, or practice, all the necessary skills they will need to improvise effectively. They have to practice finger technique, experiment with different keys, be thrust into unfamiliar musical situations and have to figure out ways to navigate them. Successful jazz musicians jettison the mindset that says "No, if I am going to play a performance, I will practice exactly what I am going to be playing." They need to flow.

How should someone train for an obstacle race the likes of which nobody had seen before? In the absence of any established plan, folks cobbled together regimens based on what they thought they might expect. But even that approach raised questions. To climb over an eight-foot wall, should you build one and practice several times per week? That's practice for the event, but is it the best training for the event? Maybe it would be better to spend part of that time doing body-weight exercises, pull-ups, grip exercises, and so on—just in case the wall was higher, inverted, or especially slippery next time. The questions were endless.

Spartan Fit! follows *Spartan Up!*, my previous book, which became a *New York Times* bestseller in the summer of 2014. This new book is a blueprint for people to follow regarding their workouts and their diets. *Spartan Fit!* will be a meaningful tool for anyone who's decided to get off the couch and get living. *Spartan Up!* inspired people to push their limits by taking on an audacious challenge. They did it, and, as a result, they developed new beliefs in themselves and their capabilities. They have hope. They have confidence. Now they're ready to make a change in how they sleep, move, and eat. *Spartan Fit!* will be their guide.

I have outlined a 30-day workout and diet plan that will take you from wherever you are to Spartan Sprint condition, meaning you will be fit to tackle our easiest race, which isn't all that easy. I intend this book to be a practical guide that will help you, the aspiring Spartan, or Spartans who want to refine their skills, to apply Spartan principles to your health and fitness. Once you're done with this book, you will have the tools needed to continue in the Spartan lifestyle on your own, and, just as important, help others achieve their own success.

"The first thirty days are all that matter," says Joe DiStefano, who with Jeff Godin, PhD, and our Training unit created the Spartan SGX certification course for Spartan trainers, athletes, and fans. "If you're setting out to train for a race, lose weight, do a pull-up — whatever you may be trying to achieve — the first thirty days will set the stage and dictate your future performance. Furthermore, it will serve as a point of reflection when the road gets bumpy and progress comes slower in the future."

The challenge of becoming Spartan Fit makes it fun, though. Fitness-wise, you have to develop a little bit of everything. This is a program for generalists, not specialists. Strength is going to be important, but so are power and muscular endurance. You must build your aerobic capacity, but you're also trying to increase your anaerobic threshold. This is where high-intensity interval training (HIIT) helps, allowing you to withstand the fatigue that sets in as you confront the obstacles between the run stages. After you experience one of those challenging obstacles mid-race, you'll recover a little bit faster than the average person if you have a good aerobic capacity. It'll also allow you to put forth as much effort as possible in the next obstacle.

This book teaches you to train for a Spartan Race, but what we've found is that Spartan training prepares you for most sports. Truthfully, the fitness regimen and dietary advice in this book can be applied to any endeavor, whether it's running, wrestling, skiing — virtually any sport you care to name. Moreover, it will prepare you for everyday life! It can help you recover from injury, heartbreak, emotional trauma, and stress.

Even if you don't want to do a race, this program is still a great way to get in shape. You may need to lose weight, and weight loss is part of the picture, but only a very small part — a by-product, really. You'll burn fat, build muscle, increase your endurance, and begin to develop obstacle immunity, meaning nothing will faze you. You'll have more energy and get rid of brain fog and depression. And yes, if you want to look great, attract a partner, and mate like an animal, this will help with that too. Your self-confidence, like your fitness, will skyrocket.

You may wonder how someone can expect to complete an endurance event as demanding as a Spartan Race after training for thirty days. I believe people are capable of heroic levels of endurance when their lives depend on it. Say your car broke down on the side of the road, and you had to walk 26.2 miles to find food and water . . . would you do it? Or would you die? I hope you would do it, but, sadly, many people in real situations just like this one do not. Hell, people on lifesaving drugs take them only 55 percent of the time, so even when there is a magic pill, often people don't take it. Poor health endangers millions of people in this country, and many of them know their lives depend on change, yet they still choose to do nothing in response. I believe a large part of the problem is that they don't know how to start.

I'm promising big changes with this book, but before you get too excited, you need to know that taking this leap is seldom easy. Following the advice I give may seem less alluring than simply sitting on the couch. But follow the Spartan Fit regimen and I believe you'll save or at least extend your life.

This fitness leap, like any drastic lifestyle change, is difficult, because humans are creatures of habit. We know when to watch our favorite shows, when to arrive at the airport to catch a flight, when to brush our teeth. We go to work on Monday and sleep in on Saturday. Some of us go to church, some watch football. We like to assume we'll eat another meal, live another day, cash another paycheck, and that nothing out of the ordinary will interrupt what we perceive to be straight and steady progress toward some goal. Often we settle into these routines lacking self-awareness, only to wake up in a strange place, blink, and say, "How did I get here? Have I been here this whole time?" Habits become deeply ingrained, and they exert a unique and powerful control over our lives that sometimes takes more than willpower to resist.

Precious few are immune to the waking sleep of habitual life. Even the best of us can become so comfortable that days blur into weeks, weeks into months, and, before we know it, we are living a life constructed for the most part while asleep. Heck, twenty years ago, when I was a trader on Wall Street, growing plump in my office chair, I had no idea what was going on with my health. I just knew I didn't feel nearly as well each day as I thought I should. Many of us are sleeping now. If we don't wake up soon, we may end up somewhere we didn't want to go, or worse, nowhere.

In sleepwalking through life, a person may unknowingly reject a golden opportunity, thinking it strange and unconventional and therefore incompatible with "normal." But could it be that "normal" is not what it should be? That the good life has gradually been covered and weighed down with something else, to the point where it is now buried? Could it be that what we *thought* was life has kept us from living this whole time? What could living be, anyway, if it's not this? So the truth startles us, unsettles us, even terrifies us, because it clashes so violently with our neat and tidy expectations and with our sense of what is normal. The truth asks too much. We'd have to change everything. Furthermore, the devices, systems, and tools we have to make our lives better are actually crippling. They are braces and casts for our mental muscles, atrophying the mind's ability to adapt and then overcome.

The habits we form become so strong that we believe change is impossible. Only, this is untrue. Change is actually a guarantee; the only variable is the form it takes. Continue with life as is, and the changes experienced will be negative: declining health, zero motivation, and lack of energy and achievement. Our limits are a prison of our own making, with bars made of a thousand small decisions to sit and wait, to accept the reality given to us by everyone but ourselves. Everything in the life of habit is predetermined. Without new horizons, we might as well call it quits.

People who are stuck in what's normal and familiar are going to quit at the first sign of discomfort. Where I see this most often is in people's lack of physical fitness. They'll work up the motivation to go to the gym one day and think, "Phew, that's enough work for one day — now I'll just go back to my smartphone or video game." But Spartans don't fear pain or exhaustion, because they know that every time they go beyond what they thought was possible, they grow stronger, braver, and greater than they were before. Improvement is motivation enough for a Spartan. We smile while all hell is breaking loose, because we know that we'll come out better on the other side.

Spartans always respect a challenge, but, beyond that, they respect their health. If life is truly important and meaningful, then health must be a top priority. Health, not gold and silver, is wealth!

Health is not merely the momentary absence of disease or injury; it's the best possible physical and mental state of a human being. When a person maximizes their health like a true Spartan, they don't just go about daily life without getting fatigued; they gain the ability to *enjoy* their life each day while being filled with a sense of wellness and capability. They fear neither distance nor height nor strain. A true Spartan is ready for anything life throws their way. The Spartan Races help develop this capability, and then validate and extend it once it has been established.

Humans are meant to strive and grow. From birth to death, trillions of cells in our body continuously reproduce and regenerate. Humans are meant to work, to sweat, and to then bask in the exhaustion that often accompanies great achievement. Humans are meant to be healthy, with a body that functions long and efficiently. Humans are meant for a greater purpose than sitting, watching, and consuming. And it's not just our physical health I'm talking about: striving and struggling give our lives deeper meaning.

No one is born physically fit. Everyone who ever became fit did so through a thousand simple decisions — decisions they made every day to move, to exercise, to purge their imperfections, to eat the healthiest foods, and to structure their lives in pursuit of important goals. You may be out of shape or in failing health, but change is still possible. When you leave the couch, it will be headfirst. Your mind leads the way; your body follows suit.

Before that moment, a thousand excuses might enter your mind:

"I don't have time."

"I'm out of shape."

"I'm scared I'll injure myself."

"This whole fitness thing is just a fad."

If you think you don't have time, you probably don't. If you think you're out of shape, you probably are. Yet for every obstacle we face, there is a solution, if only we take the time and energy to look for it. If fitness is a fad, if feeling your best every day is a fad, then human life itself is a fad. Don't worry. It will be over before you know it, and then some other species will step up to the podium and deliver its inaugural address as the new fad.

What I'm asking you to do here is to *wake up.* Turn on the lights. Get off the couch. Put down the French fries. The old normal of inactivity, of processed food, and of limits to your potential is over. A new normal is about to begin. It consists of constant improvement, of crushing your goals, and of robust living built on the most human of principles. If you have a Spartan mindset, you hit your workouts as consistently as you brush your teeth; and the unhealthy meal, not the healthy one, becomes the exception. You'll like what you see in the mirror, but you'll probably be too busy kicking ass to bother looking.

This guide is for anyone who wants to break through their limits and achieve what they thought was physically impossible. For some, that might be running a marathon. For others, it might be a walk to the grocery store. I'm not here to tell you that you're fat. I'm not here to make you into a fitness nut. I'm here to make you into a life nut, to remind you of who you are and highlight your innate potential.

Like I said, I never question whether I'll finish a race — even though there are some I didn't finish. And by the time you're Spartan Fit, you won't question your potential either. Training will take you to a point where doubt and fears of failure don't prevent you from embarking upon a new challenge. Instead, you will see your victory with a sense of certainty and even inevitability.

But first things first: get to the starting line.

We like to say "You'll know at the finish line," but there's also something you'll know at the starting line. When you're surrounded by thousands of screaming people — professional athletes and amateurs, Navy SEALs and cancer survivors, firefighters and hairdressers, men and women, young and old, people of every background. When adrenaline is coursing through your veins. When there's a little bit of fear inside you, but you're prepared to overcome any obstacle ahead. When you're Spartan Fit.

That's when you'll know that this is bigger than any race.

It's a way of life and a movement.

2

THE LEGEND OF SPARTA

"Go tell the Spartans, stranger passing by,
that here obedient to their laws we lie."

— EPITAPH TO FALLEN SPARTANS
AT THE BATTLE OF THERMOPYLAE

LIFE IS GOOD in Santa Monica, California.

The sun is almost always shining; the temperature drifts lazily in the sixties and seventies all year round; the humidity isn't bad; and the beaches are as golden and well manicured as the bodies.

I could never live there.

Life is *too* good, *too* predictable, *too* easy. But it's a nice place to visit.

I was walking on the beach that stretches from Santa Monica to Venice, which is home to one of the most famous places in modern fitness: Muscle Beach. It started in the 1930s with outdoor gymnastics, and a bodybuilding platform soon followed. The outdoor bodybuilding space — the original Muscle Beach — moved from the Santa Monica Pier to Venice Beach, where today you can still see bulky bodybuilders doing curls. A little ways down you can still see outdoor gymnastics. An unassuming woman grabs the rings, then powerfully and gracefully swings from one to the next. Nearby some dreadlocked surfers balance on slacklines. A couple boys wrestle in the sand.

It's a pretty cool scene. And I guarantee you that the lean, strong gymnasts and surfers would crush the showboating bodybuilders in an obstacle race.

Only a few blocks away — on Second Street in Santa Monica — is where fitness pioneer Vic Tanny opened a health club in 1939. It would become the first nationwide gym chain. Vic Tanny basically invented what people now call a "gym": indoor spaces with carpeting, mirrors, and easy-to-use equipment — even the monthly installment plan and aggressive sales tactics. I fucking hate to see gyms that are nothing more than depressing dungeons.

The word "gym" is short for "gymnasium" — the outdoor athletic complexes where ancient Greeks used to train, socialize, and learn. The true gym isn't rows of free weights, "machines," and unoccupied treadmills in a strip mall; it's all these people outside playing and training together — running, jumping, swinging, balancing, wrestling, and then going for a nice cold swim. In fact, the Greek word *gymnos* meant "naked," and the gymnasium was the place where ancient Greeks would train in the buff. I looked around at all the nearly naked people on the California beach — not much has changed. Maybe the ancient Greeks were on to something.

After all, the ancient Greeks invented the Olympics. Every four years, all the warring Greek city-states would declare a truce so that athletes, most of them soldiers, could travel to the host city to participate in athletic competitions.

Even though the Panhellenic culture prized athletics, there was one city-state that developed an elite warrior class who became known the world over for its athletic and military prowess: Sparta.

How did they do it?

It's not as if the Spartans were more genetically gifted relative to their close neighbors. Nor did Sparta earn its fearsome reputation from individual heroics (despite Spartans claiming to be descended from Heracles, the divine hero we know as Hercules). The modern meaning of the word "spartan" hints at the secret: 1) rigorously self-disciplined; 2) simple, frugal, austere; 3) marked by brevity of speech, laconic; 4) courageous in the face of pain, danger, or adversity. *None* of these Spartan qualities refers to brute strength, raw speed, or incredible stamina — but the Spartan way of life produced them nonetheless.

What can we learn from the ancient Spartans about their methods? To answer that question, I was about to meet up with one of my personal heroes: best-selling author Steven Pressfield. I've met a ton of interesting folks over the years, and Pressfield is one of the only people who made me feel a little starstruck. He knows more about ancient Sparta, military history, and warrior virtues than almost anyone alive.

Pressfield is the author of more than a dozen books, including *The Legend of Bagger Vance* (on golf), *The War of Art* (on writing), *The Warrior Ethos* (on martial values), and one of my all-time favorites, *Gates of Fire.* That historical novel is an epic retelling of the Battle of Thermopylae, when King Leonidas and his three hundred Spartans sacrificed their lives to hold off the Persian hordes while the Greek city-states marshaled a larger force. Pressfield is a former Marine, and his book has become required reading at West Point, the U.S. Naval Academy, and the Marine Corps Basic School at Quantico.

It was about 9 a.m. when Pressfield and I met up on the beach. He's now in his seventies, and his hair is white, but he still has a Marine's firm handshake. After some chitchat, we got down to business.

"You could have written about anything, but you chose the Spartans. How did that happen?" I asked him.

"You know, Joe, I'm kind of a believer that a book chooses you. There was a passage in Herodotus about Dienekes, the bravest of all Spartans at the pass of Thermopylae. He was told that when the Persians fire their arrows, they're so numerous that they block out the sun. And Dienekes said, 'Good. We'll have our battle in the shade.' When I read that, I felt like I knew that guy."

I remembered that line from the movie *300*, which came out nearly 2,500 years after Herodotus wrote down that passage.

"The Spartans got a bad rap throughout history," Pressfield continued. "Everybody always talks about the Athenians, who built the Parthenon and la-dee-da-dee-da, right? And the Spartans were always portrayed as these brutish thugs who beat everybody up and have no sense of humor. And I just thought, I want to bring a little humanity to that culture and bring it into the modern world so people can relate to it a little bit. Because I always thought it was a culture almost from another planet, it was so extreme. It just fascinated me, so I plunged in."

Maybe that's why I personally relate to the ancient Spartans so much. I do a lot of extreme stuff, and people look at me like I'm crazy. And, look, I *am* crazy — but there's more to it than that. There's a method to my madness.

"So how long did it take you to research the Spartans?"

"I don't know if you know this," Pressfield replied, "but we don't have much written by actual Spartans. Sparta was such a secret society, they concealed everything. But there is a lot of writing in the ancient world by other people — Athenians and so forth. So, I just read everything. A lot of *Gates of Fire* is my imagination projecting back into that world."

Sparta and its martial culture were very real, but its inner workings were mysterious even to the ancients, its origins wrapped in legend. Pressfield gave a quick retelling of Sparta's origin story.

"A few hundred years before Sparta became Sparta, it was just a regular Greek city-state. Didn't have that Spartan ethos. They would go to war in summer like every other city-state, and they'd get their ass kicked half the time. Then comes along this heroic figure: Lycurgus."

According to ancient historians, Lycurgus was the younger brother of the king. When the king died, Lycurgus ascended the throne only to soon give it away to his brother's newborn child. After being falsely accused of plotting to kill the child before he came of age, Lycurgus left Sparta. He spent years traveling the ancient world — Crete, Egypt, Ionia — studying forms of government and distilling lessons of statecraft from Homer and other ancient writers. In time, the Spartan people recognized their folly and pleaded for Lycurgus to return and take the throne. Upon returning, he implemented a series of reforms that touched every aspect of Spartan life — now known as the Laws of Lycurgus or the Spartan Constitution, which created the incredible Spartan legacy that lasts to this day.

"We only have a few word fragments remaining of the Spartan Constitution," Pressfield said. "Lycurgus didn't want to compel Spartans with written laws. They were passed down orally, so Spartans would have to know them by living them."

The first few reforms weren't about military preparedness, per se, they were about political equality and economic austerity. First, he introduced a council of elders to check the power of Sparta's two kings and, in some cases, the citizens. Second, he seized all the land and redistributed it to citizens in equal lots, sufficient to provide enough food for "proper fitness and health." He also tried to redistribute all physical possessions and livestock, but citizens resisted — so he outlawed gold and silver money in favor of iron (which was largely useless outside of Sparta). He banned foreign goods so that Sparta would remain self-sufficient and untainted by exotic luxuries.

Full citizens — called *Spartiates* — were an elite class of professional warriors who did not engage in commerce or manual labor and would refer to one another as peers ("equals"). The more numerous *perioikoi* ("dwellers around") were neighboring peoples who had been conquered by the Spartans and subsumed into the culture. They were free noncitizens, primarily engaged in commerce and crafts, had more freedom to travel and trade than Spartan citizens did, and fought alongside the Spartan citizen army on an equal basis. And the *helots* — most numerous of all — were subjected peoples who primarily worked the land as serfs. Scholars still debate the nature and relationship of these and other castes — for example, we know there were regular opportunities for helots to move up in the world (military service), but there was also severe brutality (mass slaughter to prevent uprisings).

To become citizens, boys had to complete the rigorous training regimen that, more than anything else, made Sparta famous in the ancient world and legendary in ours: the *agōgē*.

"A boy would enter the agoge at age seven," Pressfield said. "They'd be in their own little troop for the next decade. And the idea was that children weren't raised exclusively by parents but by everyone. Which was a little like a cross between the kibbutz movement in Israel and Army Ranger school."

The agoge was tough and only grew tougher as the boys grew older. It was designed to build resistance to hardships such as hunger, exhaustion, and physical pain — and to cultivate "smart obedience, perseverance under stress, and victory in battle." They also practiced athletic skills that would eventually prove useful in combat, such as running, throwing a javelin, and wrestling — as well as survival skills.

It is said that the boys were chronically underfed. They were encouraged to steal more food, but were violently whipped if they were caught. They usually went barefoot — a boot camp without boots. They exercised naked, and after the age of twelve were only given a single simple cloak for the entire year. They rarely bathed. They slept together on communal mattresses. They endured heat and cold, hunger and thirst, darkness and lashings. They were encouraged to fight regularly, and to take orders from leaders in their troop. And they drilled with shield, sword, and spear.

One tale has it that a test in the agoge involved a ten-mile cross-country race in which the boys, under threat of punishment, had to carry a mouthful of water without spilling a drop. One young male accidentally swallowed his water while traversing rough terrain and bit down on his own tongue in the process. Rather than spit out the blood and his jagged tongue, he waited until he had completed the course, spewing the contents of his mouth out at the feet of his instructors instead.

While it's absolutely true that the agoge was more physically and psychologically grueling than anything else in Greece, it's a myth that the agoge was exclusively focused on military training. Like other elite Greeks, the boys learned reading, writing, singing, rhetoric, and philosophy — and at a sufficiently high caliber, such that Athenian intellectuals like Xenophon sent their sons to be educated there. Some scholars also argue that the chronic underfeeding and thievery were a specific phase in the agoge rather than a full decade of deprivation. Sparta religiously observed many holidays when even soldiers wouldn't go to war; presumably the boys weren't constantly training for war either. Sparta *was* different, but it's important to remember that Spartans were human too.

The core training period lasted a decade (age seven to seventeen), at which point the boys were inducted as men into the military reserves for a few years, and then spent a decade serving in the military and living in the barracks. At age thirty they could marry, vote, and hold office.

"A rite of passage has been part of every culture throughout history, an initiation into the greater society," Pressfield said. "Plains Indians had their vision quest. Hell, gangs have their initiation rituals. But today all we really have are fraternities, sports teams, and maybe the military. It's funny, they probably had a graduation from the agoge, but I have no idea what it was. You can bet it was special."

The agoge was only one of Lycurgus's reforms; he also introduced common messes where all Spartan citizens, including kings, would eat the same meals together. The justification sounds eerily relevant: "This prevented them from spending the time at home, lying at table on expensive couches, being waited upon by confectioners and chefs, fattened up in the dark like gluttonous animals, and ruining themselves physically as well as morally, and by giving free rein to every craving and excess which demanded lengthy slumbers, warm baths, plenty of rest, and, in a sense, daily nursing."

As you might imagine, those early Spartan elites pouted and threw a temper tantrum when they weren't allowed to sit on the couch and eat ice cream — supposedly a mob attacked Lycurgus and a young man gouged out his eye.

But the mess hall system took hold. Members had to contribute staple foods like barley meal, wine, cheese, figs, money for fish or meat, and a share of anything they hunted.

The staple dish was "black broth": a liquid concoction of pig's blood, salt, and vinegar that other ancient Greeks thought was utterly disgusting. "It's gnarly!" said my friend Dean Karnazes, an ultramarathoner whose family hails from the Spartan region of Greece. He tried a local version made with barley, chopped vegetables, watered-down red wine, and goat's or pig's blood.

"Common messes were forerunners of fraternities, I'd imagine." Pressfield laughed. "Plutarch says each mess had fifteen or so men, and it took a unanimous decision to induct a new member — so any existing member could blackball you. They must have developed their own character. And you had to pay your dues in food. And the messes all lined a certain road, like fraternity row."

At night, Spartans walked home from the messes without a

torch. They were never supposed to use a light at night, in order to get used to moving "cheerfully and fearlessly" in darkness.

The doors of the mess bore an inscription —"Not a word goes out through these"— to allow them to speak openly about any subject. Boys ate at the messes so they could learn how to speak and act like grown men.

The Spartan style of speaking was notable throughout the ancient world: brief and to the point. The modern word "laconic" describes someone who uses few words, and it's derived from Laconia (or Lacedaemonia), the region of Greece ruled by Sparta. It wasn't simply that "actions speak louder than words," though that was part of it; it was that words, like actions, should be direct and effective. Spartans were known for their pithy sayings and cutting rejoinders, which speaks to their skill with language, not disdain for it.

Humor was important too — not only learning how to make a joke (and in a manner less crude than the stereotypical fraternity), but also how to take one: "For their own part they would grow used to making fun and joking without becoming indecent, as well as not taking offence when they were the butt of the joke. In fact this ability to take a joke would seem to be very Spartan."

Ancient Spartans are often portrayed as bullies, but Plutarch says they had a sense of decorum and judgment for when things went too far: "If a joke was too much for someone to take, he could plead with the person making it, and the latter left off."

Humor plays an underappreciated role in a strong military since it fosters strength, unity, and esprit de corps. First, learning how to take a joke teaches you how to be confident, not defensive. Second, humor is an equalizer: if anyone — even the king — can be the butt of a joke and everyone else is free to laugh, then it creates a sense of equality and cohesion. And third, humor in the face of danger summons courage.

"Put yourself in their place at Thermopylae," Pressfield said.

"They're waiting for this huge army of Persians to show up. How scared must they have been? Then a messenger runs up and reports the massive number of Persian archers. Every man's balls retract into his abdomen. Then Dienekes delivers his line about fighting in the shade — everyone laughs and they regain their courage. That was the whole point of humor. In a group facing the possibility of death, each man draws into his own little shell and loses the one thing keeping him brave and the group powerful: cohesion with his brothers. Laughter unites everyone; it was very inclusive."

So even though the Spartans seemed cold and terrifying to out-siders, they were almost certainly a damn funny crew among them-selves — similar to the locker room humor of a professional sports team mixed with the gallows humor of a military barracks.

Historians hammer Sparta for its lack of culture relative to rival Athens, and it's true that foreign ideas were discouraged and read-ing and writing weren't emphasized. But Spartans *were* known for their singing and lyric poetry, which modern people simply can't appreciate since it was never recorded or written down. As with humor, music and song also served a martial purpose.

"They sang as they marched into battle, as they crossed that open space to clash with the enemy," Pressfield continued. "Their music was made by pipes — you can hear them over a long distance and they created a cadence along with the songs. And singing forces your lungs to work, breaking the fear that might stop you from breathing. I'm sure it wasn't in the movies, but it was very rhyth-mic and orderly. And that would make it even more terrifying. You wouldn't see any flesh anywhere. It would look like one giant ma-chine coming toward you. And with the scarlet cloaks, burnished shields and helmets? Must have been a hell of a sight."

Humor, music, and song — Spartan war tactics.

As gloriously heroic as that may sound, the Spartans frowned on soldiers who got caught up in the passion of the battle and lost their discipline. Herodotus writes of Aristodemus, a shamed Spartan warrior who attempted to regain his honor by "rushing forward with the fury of a madman in his desire to be killed before his comrades' eyes." He was no longer considered a coward, but he received no honors for his heroics. Spartan strength came from the group, not the individual — and warriors were to fight with a desire to live, not suicidal abandon.

That may seem like a contradiction, since the Spartans were responsible for the most epically suicidal stand in military history: the Battle of Thermopylae. But there's a logic to it: if every individual was prepared to die *for the group*, the group would be more likely to prevail — and the individuals survive. The Spartans actively cultivated a suicidal reputation to put fear in their enemies.

"The quips they made never had hope in them," Pressfield said. "It's never 'Don't worry, guys, we'll survive.' It's always 'We're all fucked, but we're gonna go down swinging.'"

Everyone knows the Spartans were unmatched in their willingness to fight to the death, but few know they also had an unmatched reputation for mercy once they had won the battle. Spartans thought it dishonorable to butcher soldiers who had already surrendered. Their reputation for mercy also induced their opponents to surrender (and live) rather than fight to the end (and die). Nor did Sparta exact tribute from members of the Peloponnesian League, the alliance it led, other than soldiers in times of war. When Sparta defeated Athens in the Peloponnesian War, Sparta's allies demanded that Athens be razed and its people slaughtered. Sparta refused, honoring the role of Athens in repelling the Persian invasions — which had taken place generations prior.

"I would love to see what Sparta actually looked like," Pressfield said as he gazed into the distance. "It wasn't a walled city — they said their men were stronger than walls. It was five villages. I can't believe it *wasn't* beautiful. Simple perhaps, but beautiful. Like the playing fields of Eton — it must have been full of grassy expanses, playing fields, running tracks. I'm sure the gymnasia were beautiful, outdoors mostly, but with Greek stonework. Nothing really remains."

My mind drifted to Pittsfield, Vermont, and what we're building there.

"This is just my own instinct," Pressfield said, "but the idea of Sparta as a super-militaristic culture with nothing else — that just can't be true. It was like a phalanx: it looked damn scary from the outside but it was intimately bonded on the inside. I'm sure Sparta was beautiful, with a lot of laughter and music. And the women were supposedly the most beautiful in Greece."

Actually, in the world: Helen of Troy — also known as Helen of Sparta — was immortalized as "the face that launch'd a thousand ships" after her abduction triggered the legendary Trojan War. In Homer's *Iliad*, the Spartan king Menelaus invokes an oath sworn by all of Helen's suitors to defend her in case anyone abducted her, and his brother Agamemnon leads the combined Greek forces — including the heroes Odysseus and Achilles — to a decade-long war on the other side of the Aegean. They ultimately prove victorious, and Menelaus returns with Helen to Sparta. But Spartan women were renowned for more than their beauty.

"Women had much more freedom in Sparta than anyplace in the ancient world," Pressfield said. "Even in Athens, a pretty cosmopolitan place, women were cloistered and kept in the house. A lot of women wore veils. Pericles, the greatest Athenian statesman and general during its Golden Age, thought the best woman was an anonymous woman. Sparta was the only city where women were encouraged to exercise and be athletic."

Better treatment of women started early. The highest ideal for a Spartan woman was to bear strong sons, but it was said that female babies were equally or better fed than male babies (who were purposefully underfed). Girls were encouraged to be athletic from a young age and they received physical training in running, wrestling, the discus, and javelin. They wore attire that was more revealing — scandalous throughout Greece — but which allowed them a greater range of motion. And they appeared in athletic parades naked — not for immodest reasons, according to Plutarch, but in order to instill pride in physical fitness. Spartan girls weren't supposed to wed until they were physically ready for childbearing, whereas prepubescent girls were frequently given away in marriage throughout much of the ancient world.

Spartan women gained unprecedented power, since the men were often away on campaign. They didn't just manage the home economy, they managed the estate — and city.

"Sparta was one of the only places where women were allowed to own property," Pressfield said. "Toward the end of the Spartan heyday, women owned almost all the property, because so many men had died in battle. And the remaining men complained that the women were out of control, lording it over everybody!"

When Queen Gorgo, the wife of King Leonidas, was asked why Spartan women were the only ones who could rule over men, she famously responded: "That is because we are the only ones who give birth to men." It's one of many gritty quotations from Plutarch's *Sayings of Spartan Women*, where many mothers tell their sons to come home victorious or don't come home at all: "With your shield, or on it."

Pressfield ends *Gates of Fire* by emphasizing the role of Spartan women. It's one thing to hear Spartan soldiers praise a glorious death — an exaggeration of the traditional male role as warrior. It's another thing altogether to hear Spartan mothers insist that they'd prefer their sons dead than defeated, a seeming contradiction of the traditional female role as nurturing mother. For all the attention that Spartan warriors receive, Pressfield speculates that women buying into the Spartan system may have been the linchpin to making it all work.

This Spartan severity supposedly extended to the practice of infanticide. Plutarch says that a group of elders examined babies for any that were weak or ill-shapen, which were taken to the *Apothetae* ("place of rejection") — and thrown off a cliff. Some amount of infanticide was fairly common throughout the ancient world, but it's not clear to what extent it was actually more common in Sparta. Recent archaeological digs at the bottom of Mount Taygetus turned up a pit with a few dozen skeletons, but they were all adult or adolescent males — perhaps criminals, traitors, or prisoners — not infants.

"When I was in Sparta a few years ago," Pressfield said, "that's the only thing the people on the tourist buses wanted to see: the gorge where babies were supposedly thrown over the cliff. It was very sensationalistic."

Plutarch understood the narrative power of sensational deaths. He writes that, after instituting his reforms, Lycurgus visited the Oracle at Delphi, who had a vision that "by adhering to Lycurgus' constitution the city would enjoy the most brilliant reputation." So Lycurgus decided to sacrifice his life with "an element of distinction and effectiveness" to inspire Spartans to adhere to his laws. So he starved himself to death — and in doing so elevated himself to legend: Lycurgus the Lawgiver.

"It took a little while to catch on in Sparta," Pressfield continued, "but once it did, they stopped losing half the wars. One of the ancients said everyone agrees that the Spartan way is the best way, but no one else wants to do it."

But it didn't make sense to me that no one wanted to do it. I know millions of people who are starting to lead lives inspired by the Spartans.

"But today they're using your book in modern-day military teachings," I pointed out. "You must have struck a chord. What do you think that they're getting from the book?"

"It's probably just what you guys do at the core of your Spartan Races," Pressfield said. "It was an expression of the warrior ethos, of the concept of soldierly honor. And these days, the kind of messy wars that we're in — and I know this is true because I have a million letters and emails from guys who are in the shit — they feel like it's such a gray area that people are fighting in. It's not clear who the bad guys are, who the good guys are. So I think they respond to this story from the ancient world."

"People are lost," I agreed, "and whether they work in a cubicle or they just don't know where they are in life, or they've gotten off track, they're a little overweight, they're unhealthy, whatever it may be — and then this is a new identity. I'm a Spartan. And I can be healthy and train hard. You're not just sleepwalking through life."

"The harder it is, the more you get out of it, right? It seems counterintuitive, because why would anybody wanna go through these obstacles? But like you say, you'll know at the finish line, right? Then you'll understand."

3

AGOGE 2.0

"It is not because things are difficult that we do not dare;
it is because we do not dare that they are difficult."

—SENECA

Crunch.
One snowshoe in front of the other.
Crunch.
Step after step after step.
Crunch.
For one hundred miles.

T WAS MADNESS: 3.125 miles up the mountain; 1,000 feet of
elevation gain; 3.125 miles down the mountain; 16 times. It was
punishment from the gods: Sisyphus in snow.

Sisyphus was an ancient Greek king known for his deceitful
ways, so Zeus devised an agonizing punishment that would torture
his mind as well as his body. Sisyphus had to push a heavy boulder
to the top of a steep hill, but it would always roll to the bottom just
before he reached the summit. Over and over for all eternity.

A maddening, excruciating task that can never be completed
— that's what it felt like to Jason Jaksetic right now. At least Sisyphus knew why he was being punished, and he really had no choice
but to continue. But Jason wasn't even sure why he was punishing
himself — and he was tormented by the freedom to stop. Hell had
frozen over and he was in it.

How did he end up in Pittsfield, Vermont? Snowshoeing a hundred miles gave Jason a lot of time to think.

The previous year had been tough. Jason's hope of becoming an elite triathlete ended when he fractured his hip on his last workout before the Ironman Kentucky. After training his whole life to take that next step, it was hard for him to wake up and realize his season — and maybe his career — were over. Jason couldn't run, so he ran away — to the other side of the world. He lived a monastic, spartan existence in the remote bush of Swaziland, a tiny country in southern Africa. His home was a small hut with a concrete floor. He pumped his water by hand and transported it back home in a wheelbarrow. It was a time for him to reground and regroup, to reset his frame of reference.

And Jason did. And it worked.

When Jason returned, he walked off the plane at Newark International Airport with a renewed sense of purpose. But he had also lost an important part of his identity: his passport. The stewardess wouldn't let him back on the plane to retrieve it, so she went and grabbed it for him. He stuck it in his pocket and walked off. When Jason eventually opened the passport, he saw the unfamiliar mug of a pit bull–faced man who must have left his passport on the same plane.

The name read: *Joseph De Sena.*

Jason got home and tried to locate me. He typed my name into Google. Race results popped up. To another endurance athlete, it was a résumé — and not a bad one. *Holy shit, this guy is a maniac.* And we had even run some of the same events. Jason found a news article with a reference to Pittsfield, dialed up the general store, and got my email address. Jason returned the passport to me at my Madison Avenue office and in return he received a fateful invitation to a weekend in Pittsfield.

It was the fall of 2010 and Spartan Race had just gotten off the ground. Jason learned about the fledgling movement. I told him to sleep in the barn. The barn would become his bedroom, office, and gym — his castle and cathedral, path and passport. A few weeks later Jason packed all his earthly possessions in his car, drove up to Pittsfield, moved into the barn, and started his new job with Spartan Race.

Jason wasn't the first person whose path led to Pittsfield, and he wouldn't be the last. Matt Baatz, studying English at his local university, had been living in the barn for a year. Baatz didn't talk much about it, but he was a legend who almost single-handedly built and maintained fifty miles of Vermont trails. He sculpted a mountain with a shovel.

Everyone here was welcoming to Jason, but a lot of people come and go. Most pilgrims to Pittsfield searching for a permanent place don't make it past their first day. Too hard, too isolated, too unpredictable, too crazy. And Jason picked up on an unspoken sense that if he wanted to stay longer than a month or two, he'd have to take on a major challenge — a rite of passage.

So Jason signed up for the Peak Snowshoe Marathon — having never strapped on a pair of snowshoes. Within a day, what would have been an impressive marathon turned into an insane ultra: one hundred miles. Jason wasn't a new athlete. He'd run thirty-six miles. He'd biked four hundred miles. He'd completed several Ironman competitions, including the Ironman world championships in 2006. None of this remotely prepared him for a one-hundred-mile snowshoe race. He'd have to train in a new way.

Jason's first day on the job with Spartan Race started early. He woke up at 5 a.m. to do a few hours of office work — in the barn, of course — so he'd have time to sneak in a workout. After a 10 a.m. breakfast at the general store, he got started. His first task was to move a pile of wood. He kept his tempo up and maintained his heart rate at 145 beats per minute for an hour. Then he loaded his backpack with thirty pounds of wood, strapped on some snowshoes, and ascended to the top of the mountain. He dumped the wood at the top, sprinted to the bottom, and refilled his backpack for another ascent. He did that for two hours and fifteen minutes. Then he hit the road for a quick thirty-minute run while carrying his snowshoe gear. After this workout that lasted three hours and forty-five minutes, Jason got back to work.

It was the *Rocky IV* training montage all over again, and now Jason had played both parts. He used to be the Russian — doing hyper-specialized training with high tech equipment under controlled conditions and wearing the latest performance apparel. Now he was Rocky — training functional movements using primitive gear in harsh, variable conditions. He lived in a barn, chopped wood, dragged logs through the snow, and grew a beard (which itself grew icicles during long training days).

And before long, the race had arrived. The athletes rolled in. The town turned out. His girlfriend had arrived to support him. He was ready — or thought so.

During such a long endeavor the mind makes a journey of its own. The first loop felt easy, since Jason wasn't carrying a forty-pound pack. After two hours his mind drifted to the simple pleasure of a hot shower — not only for the physical sensation, but also to remove the smell of his own sweat and melt the ice crystals forming on his eyebrows.

At mile 13 (a little over four hours), he still felt pretty good. The next four loops were extremely challenging — more challenging than most people could endure — but it was mental and physical territory already known to endurance racers like Jason.

By mile 43, Jason was in uncharted territory. His lungs seemed clogged and he had trouble breathing, his knees were shot, and he was losing motor skills. He went inside and took a short nap.

By mile 50, Jason knew he was totally in over his head. Standing near the top of the mountain had been the moment when his confidence was revealed as naiveté.

By mile 60, Jason had learned that it was a mistake to race with a loved one present, unless that person is a paramedic or a fellow adventure racer. The damage done to your body is too intense for them to give you the support you need to get to the finish. They will ask you to stop. There will be tears and appeals to reason. But there is nothing reasonable about snowshoeing one hundred miles.

At mile 69, Jason needed food. He went inside and ate half a pizza, two Reubens, and a breakfast burrito (see page 208 for the recipe). His body was breaking down with every lap. He was the only person left on the course. Then it started to rain. The deluge eventually turned to ice, and the ice eventually turned into whiteout snow squall conditions that erased all previous footsteps more than half a foot deep in less than three hours.

After mile 81, I found Jason on the floor of the chicken coop with his face pressed into chicken shit and feathers.

"You've got to explain to me why you've been sleeping in the chicken coop," I said.

"It's fucking warm in here," he mumbled.

By mile 91, Jason was a walking catastrophe — a half-dead stumbling zombie. His right ankle was done, completely swollen, and the softened snow collapsed under the full weight of his left snowshoe on every step. Beneath the two feet of snow was a slush of water, ice, and mud. More than once he had to take his frozen fingers in soaked gloves and dig out his foot — only able to roll over on his side in exhaustion from the effort. Only to repeat the procedure a few steps later.

All sense of self had been replaced by a throbbing, ultralocalized yet nonspecific pain. The trees were taunting him, the mountain was trying to drown him.

It was dark, and a heavy snowfall had started. Jason lay down on a snow bank for what he thought would be a little nap. He looked up at the sky and understood the lunacy of his situation. And as he drifted off, he realized that he was being buried in snow. If he fell asleep, no one would miss him for three to four hours. It might be six hours before anyone actually found him. He might freeze to death. At that moment Jason realized that this wasn't a race any-more — an artificial challenge constructed to entertain suburban men battling to reclaim their masculinity. If he didn't summon the courage to get up and walk, he would die.

At mile 94 at midnight, Jason stomped into the barn from the blizzard after his longest loop yet — seven hours. He collapsed on the floor. He was done. He quit.

I was there in my winter gear and snowshoes.

"Get up. Let's go."

"You want to go for a loop with me?" Jason asked.

"Let's get it done," I said.

"I can't take another step."

"Are you pissing blood?" I asked.

"Huh?"

"Are you pissing blood?" I asked again.

"No."

"Good, then let's go."

"Let's get it done," said Jason and picked himself up.

On cue, the storm intensified. We got lost. We couldn't find the trail. We were crawling up the mountain. The streams coming down the mountain started to rise and break through the ice. We kept getting soaked when we broke through the snow. It was the opposite of self-preservation. It was madness.

When we got to the top of the mountain, Jason turned to head back down.

"Where you going?" I said. "We gotta clean up this aid station."

Jason almost lost his shit and nearly punched me. But there's a method to my madness. We were the last people on the course, and we couldn't leave the aid station a mess. So we cleaned it up. And something flipped in Jason's head and he got it. It wasn't a race anymore. There was no one watching. There were no cheering fans. There were no sponsors or endorsement deals. It was just two dudes on a mountain being crazy, cleaning up their own mess before going to bed. And we had a lot of work to do the next day.

Jason had to take off his snowshoes and crawl part of the way down. But he got it done. That's when I started to call him the Barn Beast.

Mile 100. Sixty-two hours.

Jason collapsed in the chicken coop. The old rules no longer applied. The Barn Beast was home.

Pittsfield is a mountain valley town in the dead center of Vermont. Only about five hundred people live there, and many of them only show up in winter for the skiing. The town center is tiny — maybe forty buildings with another three hundred houses scattered around the mountain. Miles of trails twist around and above the valley. You could go forty miles and not see a house. An isolated, fertile mountain valley — a little like Sparta, but with harsher winters.

I grew up in Queens, where Italian American kids like me learned grit and perseverance by working at the local businesses: a pizzeria, a cement distributor, a junkyard. I built a pool-cleaning business and then cleaned the pool of pretty much every wise guy in and around the "five families." I sharpened my elbows trading securities on Wall Street. But I wanted a more rural upbringing for my kids, where they could eat food that they had grown themselves. What if I could teach them the same principles of hard work and self-discipline through an organic farm, a bed-and-breakfast, or an obstacle race company? And there would be more space and freedom for them to train like Uma Thurman in *Kill Bill*. How cool would that be?

I didn't move there with any grand plans of sparking a movement. Just like the Barn Beast didn't plan on completing a one-hundred-mile snowshoe race, I didn't plan on building a multinational obstacle racing business. I set out on a much more personal quest: How could my wife and I inculcate a love of movement in our own children? In a time when we are undermined at every turn by junk food, technology, and modern luxury, could we build a life that encouraged strength and vitality?

Plutarch tells a story of Lycurgus, Sparta's legendary lawgiver. When pressed to make Sparta a full democracy, he responded, "Begin with your own family." Basically, if you aren't willing to experiment with your own private life, perhaps you shouldn't run a big social experiment. And if you *are* advocating a social revolution, you'd better lead by example.

Thank God I have an amazing wife. Courtney was a world-class soccer player in college. I met her during a relay triathlon on Nantucket as I was running barefoot on rocky ground in my wetsuit. She knew I was crazy; I knew she was the one. On our first date we went ocean kayaking and I aimed for a harbor in the distance; we ran out of water after the first four hours of what turned out to be an eight-hour trip. She was a true Spartan woman long before I even knew what that meant. She *is* the linchpin.

We have four wonderful children: Jack (ten), Charlie (eight), Catherine (seven), and Alexandra (three). They all passed inspection at birth, so thankfully we didn't have to throw any of them off a cliff.

The three older kids start their day at 5:45 a.m. in the barn with stretching. I'm totally insistent on stretching first and foremost as this keeps their bodies limber. Stiff, sleepy muscles need to wake up.

They have two hours of training ahead of them each day — seven days a week.

I'm not a big fan of exercise equipment and we don't have any workout machines in the barn. The kids start with bodyweight drills: bear crawls, crab walks, scorpion walks, cartwheels, back-bend flips, walking on their hands, and so on. This helps them develop strength, coordination, balance, flexibility. Maybe some wind sprints too. We have two live-in instructors who give the kids lessons in kung fu and wrestling, usually in the afternoon, which both boys have really taken to. Both disciplines teach that self-control leads to life mastery. I don't expect most families to have live-in instructors, but many parents pay for music lessons, summer camp, or even video games. We prioritize physical training in the morning — it's a habit that will pay dividends for the rest of their lives.

Then the kids eat a healthy breakfast of eggs, steel-cut oatmeal, and our own delicious riff on "black broth" (a BoKU superfood smoothie). Pancakes are an occasional treat. A nice side effect of an early morning workout? The kids get really hungry, so they don't fuss over the food we serve them. The rest of the day is easy after a hard sweat — the kids are more focused and calm, which makes parenting easier too. Days where they miss a workout just don't go as well. They're groggy, mopey, and not as well behaved.

Children have evolved to move every single day of their lives, and they *need* exercise for proper development and behavior. And if they don't exercise, don't be surprised to come home to kids who are extremely excitable — or extremely lethargic. Proper exercise creates an elevated sense of calm in their body and mind for the entire day. If more kids ran around in the morning, it'd be easier for them to focus in school — and there'd be a hell of a lot fewer kids on ADHD medications.

Kids need discipline too. They aren't good at making decisions. They haven't learned how to regulate their emotions; they can't think very far into the future; and they don't know how the world works. That's why it's hard to get them to brush their teeth — since they don't "feel" like doing it; they don't think about the long-term consequences (cavities); and they don't understand the scientific role of microbes in the mouth. Parental discipline solves all those problems.

Discipline is not about being abusive; it's about setting firm rules and boundaries and then enforcing them. And it's about the discipline in your life as much as theirs. If you make exercise as normal and inevitable as brushing their teeth, eventually kids will just start to do it too. Same with eating real food. Are exercise and nutrition any less important to a long, healthy life than brushing their teeth?

Structure is important, but it's also important for kids to have time to play in a completely unstructured way. My kids love to go in the barn, zip around on their scooters, and swing from ropes. They go outside and explore — or play games in the tree house. We do survival days when we venture farther afield and I teach them how to start fires. I wouldn't want them to do the exact same rigid, repetitive stuff every day — that's exactly what I'm against. I want them to be generalists, not specialists. Fierce little wild animals, not sad little robots.

Kids need affection too, physical and emotional. But we spoil them rotten by trying to solve every hard situation with cheap affection, a bag of candy, or a participation trophy. Helicopter parents try to avoid hard situations altogether, which is ultimately (and obviously) impossible. And I can't tell you how often divorced parents bribe their kids with candy and trinkets to seem like "the cool parent"— the kid is just a pawn in a battle among childish grown-ups. If you both love your child, *which you do,* agree to stop spoiling him or her. (That's what grandparents are for.)

Even the ancient Greeks noticed that Spartan children were

less spoiled and in better control of their emotions. Plutarch writes: "They trained children to eat up their food and not to be fussy about it, not to be frightened of the dark or of being left alone, and not to be prone to ill-bred fits of temper or crying."

Elite foreigners would even hire Spartan nurses to help raise unspoiled children — the tough-love au pair! Some things never change.

I get that I may come off as a demanding dad, and I remember chafing under my own father's heavy hand. It was my mother who opened my eyes to yoga, meditation, and wellness. My goal is to foster *internal* discipline and nurture an inherent love for athleticism. And you need parents who set the right expectations and then push kids to try new things, persevere through obstacles, and develop a level of mastery and accomplishment that will fuel a lifelong love of their endeavor. My wife and I agree on the fundamentals and we also provide a good balance.

I never stop learning, and there are always new ways to do things — for example, when I taught the kids to ski uphill. It's maybe a little unorthodox, but when you ski downhill, gravity does all the work and compensates for bad form. So I got some harnesses, put skins on my skis, and yoked the kids to me so they were facing my back as I pulled them up the hill. They leaned forward as if they were skiing and resisted as I pulled them up the hill. It was a hell of a ninety-minute workout for me — and the kids got strong and became very good skiers very fast. Taking the hard way makes everything else easier. And now we have an awesome family sport to do together.

Of course, my kids still try to duck out at times. Catherine has figured out all sorts of clever ways to skirt anything. Sometimes she reminds me of the Spartan kids who came up with clever ways to steal more food, and I've got an odd sort of respect for that. She's a great kid and she'll run a half-marathon soon. My son Jack grumbled for a while, but now exercise is just part of who he is. He's a great wrestler and competes in tournaments around the country. He ran a 50K when he was eight years old, plus the Boston Marathon.

Then my son Charlie, who was six years old at the time, started to talk about running a marathon, *so . . .*

Okay, I know pretty much everyone reading this is gonna say I'm a real asshole. But I told my wife that if Charlie gets dehydrated, we'll stop, and if not, we'll push through. And then he'll have pictures and memories of crossing the finish line of a marathon.

Charlie was ready. Two weeks before the event, he walked a half-marathon up and down the mountain in our backyard. And he'd been doing two-a-days of stretching, gymnastics, and martial arts for a while. Besides, I wouldn't want him to just run in a straight line on the pavement day in and day out. Most runners don't get injured during a marathon, they get injured "training" for a marathon — long before they ever make it to the starting line. Charlie trained in such a way that he was *capable* of running a marathon.

We faced a different obstacle getting to the starting line: seven-year-old kids aren't allowed to run the New York City Marathon. Children used to be allowed to participate — the youngest official finisher was eight-year-old Wesley Paul, who finished in an incredible three hours back in 1977. But the race introduced a minimum age limit of sixteen in 1981, then raised it to eighteen in 1988.

I respect the New York City Marathon and don't advocate breaking their rules. It's a serious race, people have spent years to prepare for that day, and you don't want to do anything foolish that would get you or anyone else injured — same as in a Spartan Race. In fact, I had decided to respect the rules and race alone. It was hard to break the news to Charlie after his hopes were so high, but it was an important lesson for him to learn.

Suddenly, there was a blinding light and I saw a young man

wearing winged sandals and the official uniform of the New York Road Runners. It was the Greek god Hermes, patron of travelers and tricksters — known for being both fleet of foot and transgressing boundaries. He alighted in front of me holding a golden lyre in one arm and Charlie in the other. "Let the boy run," he said with a wink and a grin, then deposited my smiling son in front of me and disappeared into the crowd.

Who am I to refuse the gods, especially when they are dressed as race officials?

So we ran, father and son together. We weren't trying to beat a time, just finish.

It would be a day of firsts — a world tour in 26.2 miles. In Brooklyn, we stopped for a bagel. He had never had a real Brooklyn bagel before. I chuckled when he asked me about Hasidic Jews. We continued on and ran through Queens, where he wanted to try pizza like the kind I ate growing up. He wanted to learn about the Italians who owned the pizzeria (and about their tattoos). In the Bronx, we stopped at a White Castle. He had lots of questions about the neighborhood and the tiny burgers. We ran into Manhattan and stopped for ice cream at Häagen-Dazs on the Upper East Side. "This is a nice place!" he said. Bagels, pizza, and ice cream aren't exactly what I consider nutritious options, but the experiences were more important.

Just outside Central Park, I decided to stop and see someone in medical just to be safe and make sure he was still good for the last four miles. Charlie started to cry. "Oh no," I thought, "this is awful, I'm sure these folks will think I am abusive." It turned out he was crying because he thought I was about to pull him from the course.

We finished in 5:43:27.

The time didn't matter: Charlie finished, he got it done — and it was a life-changing day for both of us. It created a new frame of reference for the rest of his life. He will never doubt that he is capable of great things, since he's already accomplished great things. Heck, at seven years he might even be the youngest person to ever run the New York City Marathon. It was unofficial, but it counts to his father, and it counts to him.

People say it's crazy that my kids train for two hours a day. But maybe it's crazy that more kids *don't* spend two hours a day doing gymnastics and martial arts — or even just playing outside. I wouldn't change a thing.

The agoge started at age seven in ancient Sparta.

It still does in Pittsfield, Vermont.

4

RACE BASICS

"The journey of a thousand miles begins with one step."
— LAO TZU

NOW THAT I'VE SCARED the shit out of you with the suicidal discipline of Spartan warriors, fighting off an armed assailant while bound and blindfolded, one-hundred-mile snowshoe races, the *Rocky IV* training montage, and seven-year-olds running the New York City Marathon, I'm here to say: You can do this.

Spartan Races are designed to test the limits of their participants, but everyone's limits are different. That's why we've created four distinct versions of the race: to challenge everyone, no matter their level of fitness. The purpose of this chapter is to offer a general sense of what each race entails, in order to give you the confidence to sign up for a race — and then, with the chapters that follow, you'll know how to train for it.

Remember, getting to the starting line is harder than getting to the finish line.

So let's get to the starting line.

THE RACES

As the name suggests, Spartan Races are *races*. They are timed, and racers are judged. A typical race has around 10,000 participants, and a few hundred people will start the course every fifteen minutes. Allow anybody to pass you, and show support for everybody.

The four types of races differ primarily in length and number of obstacles. If racers fail to complete an obstacle, they are hit with a penalty — usually thirty burpees that must be completed before they can move on. Any racer who doesn't complete these burpees is disqualified.

SPARTAN SPRINT (3+ MILES, 20+ OBSTACLES)

The Spartan Sprint, the shortest of the four, is manageable for beginners yet still capable of challenging even seasoned athletes, who might be encountering some of the obstacles for the first time. It covers three-plus miles on varied terrain and includes twenty or more obstacles. There's plenty to test an elite athlete, but lots of beginners go at their own pace, and that's fine. The fastest times for the Spartan Sprint are under thirty minutes, the average time is around one hour, and the slowest times are two hours or more.

SPARTAN SUPER (8+ MILES, 25+ OBSTACLES)

The Spartan Super covers eight-plus miles of rough terrain with twenty-five or more obstacles. The Super is designed for those with more athletic experience who want to put their physical stamina and mental resolve to a unique test. It's extremely hard, no matter your fitness level — and it's likely to push you to your limits.

SPARTAN BEAST (13+ MILES, 30+ OBSTACLES)

The Spartan Beast is designed for seasoned athletes who want to come face-to-face with their demons. It covers thirteen-plus miles of insane terrain with thirty or more obstacles. The Beast is a half-marathon from hell.

SPARTAN ULTRA BEAST (26+ MILES, ?? OBSTACLES)

Every Spartan Race is a baptism; the Ultra Beast is an exorcism. It covers twenty-six-plus miles and more obstacles than you'll be able to count. There is no map or details for the course. There will be surprises, so expect the unexpected. It's much harder than running a marathon, and most people are not prepared to complete an Ultra Beast.

JR. VARSITY AND VARSITY

For kids, we offer Jr. Varsity and Varsity races that have an emphasis on teamwork, fun, and getting muddy. The Jr. Varsity is a half-mile race for kids age four to eight. The Varsity is a mile-long race for kids age nine to thirteen.

SPARTAN TRIFECTA

No matter your fitness level, each Spartan course presents its own challenges. And those who finish a Spartan Sprint, Super, and Beast in the same calendar year will earn their Trifecta medal.

THE OBSTACLES

A Spartan Race tests the entire body with a wide range of obstacles. Below are some of the core obstacles that you'll find on our courses.

It may be tempting to train specifically for each obstacle, but the goal is to train for *any* obstacle. The way to do that isn't to train for every imaginable scenario. That would be impossible, and your training would become so rudderless as to be useless. Instead, Spartan training develops a series of physical attributes — endurance, strength, athleticism — that can be recruited in almost every situation. When combined in a training program that includes recovery, nutrition, and the mindset and code of a Spartan, you'll be prepared to overcome these obstacles and any others in your way.

A tip from the pros: it's better to stop and think about an obstacle than to fail one. Similarly, don't let the excitement of the race cause you to burn out right away. Start slower, then increase your speed, and really go hard from halfway to the finish.

ATLAS CARRY

A staple of strongman competitions, this obstacle tests your strength endurance first and foremost. You'll deadlift or snatch a heavy stone and then carry it for a short distance — just long enough to make your core scream. Everyone from a mom juggling her kid and a bag of groceries to a fireman lugging a body from a burning building is doing a variation on the Atlas carry.

Instructions:
- Pick up the stone at start flag.
- Carry it to the opposite flag.
- Put stone down.

- Do 5 burpees.
- Return stone to start flag.

Failure Modes:
- Anyone not able to move the stone to opposite flag and back to start flag.
- Elite racers who help one another.
- Anyone who doesn't complete 5 correct burpees.

Failure Penalty: 30 burpees.

BARBED WIRE CRAWL

Stay low and crawl or even roll as quickly as possible — the goal is to make it through the barbed wire crawl without scratches across your back. I hope you've been doing your bear crawls, crab walks, and other animal movements. Those will help you survive through this obstacle. There's not a lot of teamwork involved in this one. You're kind of on your own.

Instructions:
- Crawl under the barbed wire. (Rolling *is* allowed.)
- Packs and bottles must go through the barbed wire obstacle.
- No diving.

Failure Modes:
- Skipping the obstacle.
- Failure to carry personal belongings through the obstacle.
- Going over wire or cord designed for passing under (unless obstacle is damaged).

Failure Penalty: Disqualification.

BUCKET BRIGADE

Bucket Brigade is designed to wear down your whole body. Fill the bucket with gravel and trek the prescribed route. A grueling task with a special stipulation: if you don't come back with all the gravel in your bucket, run the obstacle again.

Instructions:

- Fill the bucket with gravel from the bin to a point above the line of holes in the bucket.
- Carry the bucket along the prescribed route.
- Return filled so that all holes are covered with gravel.
- Empty bucket back into the bin upon completion of the obstacle route.
- Return bucket to start flag.

Failure Modes:

- Failure to return to the line with a full bucket.
- Carrying bucket on shoulders, neck, or head.
- Failure to empty the bucket into the bin.

Failure Penalty: Repeat the obstacle.

HERCULES HOIST

Anchor yourself to the ground, grab on to the rope with your iron grip, and start pulling. Once that weight is at the top, you must lower it slowly. If the weight slams to the ground, you owe me 30 burpees.

Instructions:
- Pull the rope to raise the weight until the knot or weight reaches the top.
- Lower the weight slowly and with control, without releasing the rope, until weight reaches the ground.

Failure Modes:
- Failure to fully raise the weight.
- Dropping the weight.
- Elite racers who help one another.

Failure Penalty: 30 burpees.

MONKEY NET

Bringing back a favorite childhood obstacle with a twist, the cargo monkey net has been burpee town for many a Spartan. Don't stop moving until you ring that bell at the end!

Instructions:
- Cross the net using only your hands, and ring the bell on the other side.
- Racers are not allowed on top of the obstacle.
- Feet are allowed to ring the bell only if athlete chooses that method.

Failure Modes:
- Falling from net.
- Feet touching net above head.

Failure Penalty: 30 burpees.

ROPE CLIMB

You've climbed a rope before — in fourth-grade gym class. Try it now sixteen feet up on a rope caked with mud, sweat, water, and Spartan blood (okay, maybe not blood). We recommend hooking your foot in some variation to stabilize yourself as you race to the top. Fearful of heights? Suck it up and don't look down.

Instructions:
- Climb the rope. Ring the bell.

Failure Modes:
- Failure to ascend the rope.
- Failure to ring the bell.
- Use of mechanical assistance.

Failure Penalty: 30 burpees.

SPEAR THROW

Unleash your inner Spartan at our trademark obstacle. You will need a steady hand and a strong arm as you let fly!

Instructions:
- You have one attempt to throw the spear and have it stick into the spearman (wood or hay).
- The spear cannot touch the ground.

Failure Modes:
- Spear does not stick into the spearman or it is touching the ground.

Failure Penalty: 30 burpees.

TIRE DRAG

An iron grip will be necessary to conquer the tire drag. Pull-ups and many variations of rowing exercises will help you prepare for this grueling obstacle.

Instructions:
- Pull the tire out until the line is taut, grabbing only tire.
- Return to the rope attachment point (stake), sit, (butt must be on the ground), and pull the tire back to the stake using the rope.
- In some events order may be reversed (pulling first, followed by dragging).
- Athlete may not carry tire.
- Tire must be touching the ground at all times.

Failure Modes:
- Unable to complete task.
- Not pulling the tire out until the rope is taut. (Redo or fail.)
- Not pulling the tire all the way back. (Redo or fail.)

Failure Penalty: 30 burpees.

TRAVERSE WALL

Rock climbers will feel right at home with the small handholds and footholds — everyone else will want this gauntlet to end as quickly as possible. Hold on tight, stay close to the wall, and pick your spot.

Instructions:

- Traverse the wall using only the handholds and footholds. Ring the bell.

Failure Modes:

- Touching the ground after start.
- Touching the top of the wall after start.
- Failure to ring the bell.
- Use of mechanical assistance.

Failure Penalty: 30 burpees.

WALL JUMP

May we recommend a running start? Getting up and over our walls takes upper-body strength of the sort forged by pull-ups, dips, and other body-weight moves. Once you reach the top of the wall, really try to control your descent. Graceful landing optional.

Instructions:
- Climb up and over the wall.

Failure Modes:
- Use of support structure.
- Use of kicker block by men.
- Elite racers who help one another.

Failure Penalty: 30 burpees.

Some obstacles may or may not be a part of a given race. We like to keep our races somewhat unpredictable so that you can practice conquering the unexpected. We might even throw in an obstacle that no one has seen before, just to trip you up. True Spartans build obstacle immunity, meaning, the ability to overcome any obstacle in their path, no matter what it is.

RACE PREP

COURSE CONDITIONS

Weather and course conditions are obstacles that even we can't entirely control. Suffice it to say that the conditions of any Spartan Race will be difficult. Races are held in heat, cold, snow, rain, or any combination thereof. The ground beneath your feet will be slippery with mud, uneven, and full of rocks and roots, which becomes even more daunting on steep inclines. You might wade through waist-deep water or knee-deep, shoe-stealing muck. Every course will give you at least one twist or turn that makes you say, "You've got to be kidding."

Mud plays multiple roles in our races. First, it's an added physical obstacle. It's slippery. It's sticky. It's heavy when it sinks into your shoes. If you wear glasses (we recommend contact lenses), it can obstruct your vision. Second, whereas kids instinctively want to roll around in mud, getting muddy is uncomfortable for adults in today's sanitized society. Our races force people to say good-bye to their love of cleanliness, bleached-white clothes, and spotless skin. This can be difficult for a lot of people, making mud a psychological obstacle, too. Lastly, for many people, Spartan Races are a significant rite of passage; you might call it baptism by mud.

GEAR

Don't wear anything particularly valuable on the course, because the mud has been known to claim wedding rings and other valuables. Nor should you waste your money on gimmicky gear — a shirt, shoes, and shorts are all you need. Don't wear expensive shoes that you don't want to take home caked with mud. Come to think of it, if you care about it, don't wear it. Clothes will be soaked, ripped, and stained with your own blood, sweat, and tears. If you're going to wear something, follow the example of the ancient Spartans and wear red. The blood will be harder to see.

At Spartan Race, we treat obstacle racing as a real sport. For that reason, we discourage costumes and face paint. This is a major athletic event, so don't dress like you're attending a Renaissance fair. Besides, it's in your best interest to minimize your outfit. If you came dressed in a full banana costume, you'd probably overheat, get stuck in the barbed wire, drown in your own sweat, get hypothermia, or catch on fire. Nobody has time for that, so spare yourself the embarrassment and race like a champion.

In terms of rules, common sense prevails. Every Spartan Race is governed by strict policies on gear:

- Clothing must be socially acceptable by local norms.
- Clothing must not be used in any way to assist a racer's efforts (e.g., it may not be used as a rope when climbing, or as a sail when swimming).
- No glass of any kind on the course.
- No weapons or highly flammable or explosive substances.
- Food and drink carried on the course may not contain alcohol or other mind-altering substances.
- Carry in, carry out. Leave nothing behind. Infractions will be penalized at race officials' discretion, minimum 30 burpees.

SPARTAN UP!

I asked ultramarathoner Dean Karnazes what advice he would offer to people who are thinking about taking on a new challenge.

"They're stuck on the couch, eating a pizza, watching *Oprah*. They're not motivated," I said. "Or they're doing okay but they're just not getting ahead, they feel like they're in quicksand. What can we learn from long distance running?"

"One is to set goals," Dean said. "When I talk to runners, and they say, 'I'm thinking about running a marathon' — you could hear that for years, right? Put some skin in the game. Sign up for an event. Put money on the table. Then email all your friends and say, 'I'm running this, and I'm running it for charity.' Pick a charity you admire. And that puts some pressure on you, 'cause when you want to come home and have some pizza and drink a beer, you think 'I've got a marathon coming up.' So you get after it.

"Now you're on the hook."

The only way to arrive at that starting line is self-imposed pressure. You have to say you're going to do it, and you have to promise it to enough friends that you are bound to your word. If you back out then, you just look like a fool.

That last part — finding a reason to race — is key. We encourage Spartans to share "why I race" (#WhyIRace). You need to find that purpose — whether it's a charity, a loved one, or a personal goal.

No one is going to do it for you. So go to Spartan.com and sign up.

And we'll see you at the starting line.

5

THE SEVEN PILLARS

"Everything should be made as simple as possible, but no simpler."

— ALBERT EINSTEIN

NLIKE SPECIALIZED ATHLETIC competitions, every Spartan Race is designed to test generalized fitness and adaptability to novel obstacles. So how do you train for that?

To become a well-rounded athlete requires a well-rounded training program and a holistic approach to healthy living. Spartan SGX training focuses on seven pillars — endurance, strength, athleticism, recovery, nutrition, mind, and code — that we believe comprise the essential elements of training. You'll notice that all seven of these pillars appear in the 30-Day Plan, and they're all there for a reason.

Master these and master anything.

1. ENDURANCE

"Come what may, all bad fortune is to be conquered by endurance."

— VIRGIL

The human body is adapted to run long distances. Anthropologists believe that five to seven million years ago, a hairy ancestor of both chimps and humans roamed the earth. Our ancestors gradually walked on two feet, then eventually ran upright. We lost our heavy coat of hair and gained sweat glands all over our body — all the better to hunt and scavenge under the hot African sun. Humans aren't just endurance athletes, we're endurance *animals.*

Endurance, in its most abstract sense, is the ability to sustain physical activity for long periods of time. A more practical definition of endurance is the ability to move over long distances — whether walking, running, or swimming.

Endurance requires sustained energy. Having adapted over eons, the human body has three ways of using energy to move: the immediate energy system, the glycolytic energy system, and the oxidative energy system. We can lump these into two categories: those requiring oxygen (aerobic) and those not requiring oxygen (anaerobic). The anaerobic systems fuel shorter bursts of higher-intensity movement like lifting a heavy weight or sprinting; the aerobic system and your cardiovascular fitness fuel sustained, lower-intensity movement like running from obstacle to obstacle. We designed the 30-Day Plan to train both systems, with a combination of high-intensity interval training (HIIT) and long, slow endurance days.

But there's no way to get around it — obstacle racing involves a lot of running. And if you want to be competitive, you have to cover long distances quickly. You might be ripped to the bone or be the World's Strongest Man, but ultimately your feet need to take you from the starting line to the finish line.

In my experience, wet, blistered, and hurt feet force more people to quit than their cardiovascular fitness or the obstacles. The weak link may be your feet, not your aerobic capacity — so the sooner you can strengthen your feet, the less likely that they'll fail as a result. Sometimes I'll get my shoes wet and sand-filled on purpose, embracing the discomfort to come. I'm recalibrating my frame of reference. Perhaps it's no coincidence that my feet haven't failed me yet during races.

That's why I also encourage you to be barefoot for a lot of low-intensity movement — standing, walking, and the occasional work-out — though I don't recommend rushing into high-intensity training or competing barefoot. I've run barefoot many times over the years, and I love it. This trend was sparked largely by my friend Christopher McDougall's book *Born to Run,* which highlights populations like Mexico's Tarahumara, a native population whose members ran for thousands of years without the benefits of fancy, expensive running shoes. There's a lot to learn from our misguided dependence on over-engineered running shoes, especially learning to run with a gentler, forefoot strike. Increasing time spent barefoot is definitely beneficial — especially for children — but barefoot running takes forethought, patience, and months (if not years) of practice.

Beyond racing, running has much to recommend it. You don't need expensive gear like you do with, say, skiing or cycling. Running is also meditative — nothing focuses the mind like a long run. You're not talking, you're not thinking, and you're not being distracted. It's just you and the pavement or dirt for mile after mile.

Don't just run out the door, though. Be smart about it, and maximize your running experience by following a few tips.

1) Warm up first, cool down last.

A five-to-ten-minute warm-up prepares your body for the real work to come. Your heart rate will rise gradually, rather than going from 75 or 80 heartbeats straight up to 160 per minute. Your lungs will slowly begin working harder. Your heart will send more blood to your muscles. Ideally, the farther you're planning to run, the longer your warm-up should last.

After finishing your run, cool down. If you finish a five-mile run and then just stop, blood might pool in your legs, leaving you faint. Better to finish those five miles and then walk a bit before coming to a stop. Give your body a chance to realize what's going on. After a run, I like to stretch, lie on my back with my legs elevated, and later sit in an ice tub for fifteen minutes. This all helps restore my tired body.

2) Start gradually.

Increasing your running distances slowly and steadily produces better long-term results than looking for shortcuts. I once ran three ultramarathons in one week, but it took me a long time to reach the point where I could even contemplate attempting such a crazy feat. Long before that, I started with a three-mile run that had me feeling sick and exhausted as overweight competitors trucked past me. I can still remember thinking, after only one mile, "This is hell." It's amazing that I developed so much strength and endurance after such an embarrassing start. You can too.

Aim to run 10 percent farther each week. Doing so allows your body to adapt to new demands. You wouldn't expect to bench-press seventy-five pounds on Monday and then two hundred pounds on

Friday, would you? Don't expect to make a similar leap with your running.

3) Go easy on easy runs.

This may sound strange, but many people don't run slowly enough. Eight out of every ten runs should be a minute or so slower than your target race time. If you're breathing hard in these runs, slow down until you aren't. This will ensure you're not pushing above your aerobic threshold into anaerobic territory. As the length of your runs increases, your heart and lungs may adapt more quickly than your muscles, tendons, and bones. Regularly running at an easy pace gives your skeleton and muscles the chance to catch up with your cardiovascular improvements. Your body needs to be all systems go, not some systems go.

4) Go fast on fast runs.

Sometimes you just have to push the pace. Fast runs build up cardiovascular strength by making your heart work at a high rate to deliver oxygen to the muscles in your legs. This, in turn, makes your legs stronger and more efficient at extracting oxygen from your blood. And you'd be surprised how often the barrier to progress is psychological. For years pundits said it wasn't humanly possible to run a sub-four-minute mile, then Roger Bannister did so in 1954. Just forty-six days later, John Landy broke Bannister's record — and now that's a standard for elite runners.

It can help to run with someone who is faster than you are. One day, after a solid warm-up, go at a race pace for your first three to five miles and then pull in the reins and ease into a more conversational pace — meaning, you can talk while running — for the remainder of your run. Alternatively, do the reverse. After warming up, take the first three-quarters of your run at a conversational pace. Then, for the last quarter, drop the hammer and go.

5) Head for the hills.

Hills are ideal for building muscle memory, leg strength, aerobic capacity, and running efficiency. At least once a week, dominate the hilliest route you know. My favorite uphill run is a stone staircase near my home in Pittsfield, Vermont. It's one mile straight up, an elevation gain of 1,000 feet. It takes me eleven minutes to finish it on a really good day. Needless to say, it took me a long time to build up to that pace. Don't be discouraged if you live in a flat area. Staircases work just as well as hills.

6) Take rest days at their name.

Pushing yourself is essential for developing endurance and strength, but lack of rest is a surefire way to get burned out. Endurance addicts like me tend to become obsessed, and it's easy to train excessively with our mindset. It's happened to me on more than one occasion. I've learned that you don't need to go full bore on every run. Only 20 percent of your training week should be dedicated to training at what I would call "puke-level" running (which should be self-explanatory). Sixty percent should be intense — but not too intense. Twenty percent of the week or more should be very easy training, or at least easy by Spartan standards. A leisurely jog or hike will do the trick. Know when to shut it down completely, too. Your body uses sleep and rest to rebuild torn muscles and grow stronger; in turn, this leads to less fatigue and the ability to run farther and faster.

7) Cross-training will make you a better runner.

While you're pounding the sidewalks, tracks, and trails, those surfaces are just fine; it's your joints and connective tissues taking the abuse. So don't hesitate to take a break from running and do something else that works your heart and lungs with equal intensity. Yoga, Pilates, swimming, cycling, elliptical training, rowing — the options are nearly endless. Even anaerobic strength training (especially with short intervals) can translate into aerobic gains. Swimming is especially good for helping you become a better runner, because it's low-impact, full-body resistance training combined with a demanding cardio workout.

8) Improvise—but only when you're ready.

Whether it's running, bodybuilding, or some other fitness endeavor, ideally you should start out following a plan. Only after mastering the basics should you begin to improvise. Think about music: jazz players are professional improvisers but they still started with the basic chords and sequences. But what does improvisation have to do with running? Experienced runners are prone to becoming slaves to their watches and regular routes. To mix it up, one day think distance and forget about time. Another day, time yourself and disregard distance. Throw on a weight vest to add resistance or do ten burpees every mile. Run on a different surface or under different weather conditions (in the heat, cold, or rain). Before or after running, add a twenty-minute session that includes planks, bodyweight squats, burpees, leg lifts, and crunches. The possibilities are nearly endless.

9) To improve, you must track your progress.

Making progress is often as much psychological as it is physical, and tracking your progress helps you know how hard or far to push. If you go too easy on hard runs or too hard on easy runs, then you won't break through whatever barrier separates you from the next level. Time, distance, and heart rate are typical ways to track yourself. Or, to measure your intensity, rattle off a sentence or two while you are running. If you can speak without gasping for air, pick up speed. If you can't speak, slow down.

10) Embrace the taper.

Get used to running at a race pace before tapering. Three weeks out from a race, shorten the distance of your runs by 25 to 50 percent while maintaining your goal pace for race day. I learned this lesson the hard way. I can't tell you how many times I pushed myself to the max right up to event day, only to feel exhausted at the starting line. Don't worry, you won't lose your edge by cutting back. A study conducted at Ball State University found that those reducing their mileage yet keeping the pace in their taper before race day sacrificed no cardiovascular fitness. What's more, they gained muscle strength and scored improved race times.

11) Run for a reason.

Don't just run like you're on a treadmill — run with purpose. Run through a new part of town. Run to get somewhere you need to go. Run for longer than you ever have before. Run because your partner will be proud of you. Run because the guy at work laughed at the suggestion of your doing a half-marathon and now you have a chip on your shoulder. Run because it's a beautiful day. Run because it's a cold and rainy day, and you enjoy the look of respect people give you. Run with a friend. Run through a beautiful park. Ditch your headphones and run as silently as possible, listening to the birds chattering and crickets chirping, the swish that trees make in the wind. Run because you love to run.

2. STRENGTH

"One who gains strength by overcoming obstacles possesses
the only strength which can overcome adversity."

— ALBERT SCHWEITZER

Strength is the muscular capacity to move heavy objects.

Luckily, the human body is itself a heavy object, and so you
are already equipped with most of the requisite gear for gaining
strength. Spartan strength training primarily relies on body-weight
exercises, an emphasis that differentiates us from many other approaches. Mother Nature has already provided you with a gym. Occasionally, we'll ask you to pick up a rock that you find in the woods,
but we won't ask you to isolate specific muscles to lift huge pieces of
metal that were made in a foundry.

You might think that a lack of equipment would cap the kind
of strength gains you can make with body-weight exercises. For
example, you can't keep loading on weight like you can a bench
press. Yet the reality is that each body-weight exercise can be made
more difficult than it first appears. Two elements, leverage and in-
stability, can enhance almost any exercise. Compare an ordinary
pushup to a decline pushup, then try a handstand pushup. Still
think you're not being challenged? Then do a handstand pushup
on an unstable surface. Aroo! This increasing degree of difficulty
leads to progressive overload, which is the gradual increase of
stress placed upon the body during training that leads to strength
gains.

Several different mechanisms cause muscle growth (hypertrophy):

- Cell swelling, which is "the pump"
- Metabolic stress, or the buildup of lactate hydrogen ions
- Motor unit recruitment
- Muscle tension, meaning the actual weight or load on the muscle

With body-weight training, you can easily target three of those four mechanisms of hypertrophy. If you're doing the body-weight exercises explosively and using short rest periods, you can build up enough metabolic stress to achieve a pump. If you go to failure, even if it takes you thirty reps, you'll get some motor unit recruitment and recruit fast-twitch fibers, which are involved heavily in muscle growth. Once you move into the range of fifty to one hundred repetitions, you're dealing less with those mechanisms of hypertrophy and more with endurance training. So if you can stay within that rep range from twelve to thirty reps, you can still get metabolic stress; you can still get cell swelling; and, if you go to absolute failure, you can still get motor unit recruitment, which means you can still achieve hypertrophy. You're missing only the tension component, the muscle damage you get from lifting weights.

To strength-train for a Spartan Race, it's important to focus on basic exercises that target all or at least most of your muscle groups simultaneously. The goal is to increase lactate and other factors by targeting your fast-twitch muscle fibers. This can be done by performing the exercises a little bit more explosively than you normally might. Remember, fast-twitch fibers are the ones that'll give you metabolic stress and cell swelling. In contrast, if you're using only your body weight, and you do the moves in a slow and controlled manner, you're only going to recruit the slow-twitch muscle fibers.

I recommend basic exercises like the body-weight squat. The squat is probably the most important exercise ever invented, and it's certainly a foundational movement for Spartan Race. It's basic, effective, and functional — there's a reason we recently ran a #Spartan30 squat challenge on our Facebook page. You can't really prepare for a Spartan Race without mastering the squat and then doing a bunch of them!

For the upper body, moves like a pushup, perhaps with a clap at the midpoint, will develop muscle and strength. It's a move that can literally be done anytime, anywhere, by anyone. Spartan Racers often will do handstand pushups against a wall, taxing their shoulders, their core, and everything in between them.

Another way to perform body-weight exercises and generate the sort of metabolic stress needed for muscle growth is to arrange them in what are called "complexes." A complex might be arranged like this:

Complete X rounds of:
- Split squat, twelve reps per side
- Forward lunge
- Rear lunge
- Jump squat

By the time you've completed all the rounds of this complex, you should have achieved the metabolic stress and cell swelling necessary for muscle growth to occur. As an added benefit, this training style melts body fat like butter.

Another way to achieve metabolic stress and cell swelling without dumbbells and barbells is through the assistance of a training partner. For example, you can do lateral raises with resistance from a training partner replacing the weight.

Take your body weight and mimic the tried-and-true gym exercises. Do partner-assisted resistance. Do complexes that build up metabolic stress. Do explosive movements like jump squats or clap pushups. So long as you activate those mechanisms mentioned above, you'll still be able to adapt and improve.

Most of the benefits of body-weight exercises will improve other components of overall fitness, but their chief gain will be in strength. With the strength you develop from body-weight exercises, you'll become a master of the Spartan obstacles that involve moving your body weight. You'll crush burpees and soar across the monkey bars. The easier it becomes for you to lift your own body weight, the easier it will be to perform any kind of body movement. In a way, your strength makes you weightless.

Everyone, even a Himalayan Sherpa, reaches a limit — that point at which you are D-O-N-E. Muscle fibers have been worked so hard and for so long that they will no longer fire. You killed two hundred pushups and nearly as many burpees, but now, you can no longer do another rep of either exercise. Your pectoral muscles are so fried that you couldn't lift a Q-tip to your ear.

Stamina is the ability to sustain the output of muscular force for an extended period of time. When most people think of endurance, they think of aerobic endurance, but there's a different sort of endurance, and it involves your skeletal muscle tissue, not your heart and lungs. This endurance likely varies by muscle too. You might have good local muscle endurance in your arms, allowing you to lift something many times, but also have poor muscle endurance in your legs.

One of the signature obstacles in a Spartan Race is the rope climb, as challenging a test of stamina as you're likely to encounter. So how do you train for this obstacle? Should you climb rope, to the extent that you can, or do you work on exercises that will *help* you climb rope? In other words, how specific should your training be to the event itself? The rope climb is technique-dependent, but it's limited by grip and upper-body strength. Think of it as a continuum. If you're largely untrained, you should focus on general fitness. Once you're fit, work on sport specificity and rope-climbing techniques.

Aside from rope climbing, stamina is essential for competing in a Spartan Race for one obvious reason: the burpees. If you struggle to pump out thirty burpees, every penalty is going to extend your race time. But stamina is also necessary for the notorious hill climbs, which require maximal force from your butt, calves, quads, and hamstrings for up to a mile. The sandbag carry will test these same muscles again, except you'll need to exert more force with each step to compensate for the extra weight. Finally, crawling through mud on your hands and knees is going to test your core, arms, and hip flexors as you push and pull yourself across the slippery terrain.

All these activities test you to the core of your very being. That's the whole idea, in fact! We want to push your limits in your training and then again in the race so that when you find yourself in a situation like that wrestler in the prologue, you come out on top rather than succumbing to what might even be a life-or-death situation.

I've found that putting slower, longer sessions into your training regimen can help build incredible physical and mental endurance. This type of training will advance all other aspects of your physiology. Your body will start to need less fluid, less food, and your mind will become stronger too. In other words, it's not just about doing thirty reps or running for an hour. Taking your physiology to the next level, an elite level, will require sprinkling in some eight-hour training days that are torture tests. It could be eight hours of hiking, or eight hours of kayaking or whatever, but that is how the structure of your body builds the kind of strength needed to compete. Those long days don't just build muscle — they also strengthen connective tissues like tendons and ligaments. You are not at race pace, you are just trying to be on your feet or moving for a long period of time, enough time for your entire being to say, "Get me home!" A chain is only as strong as its weakest link, and when that link breaks, you are most likely done. I have found that adding one long day a week for five weeks straight leaves your body ready for anything.

Bodybuilders lack this type of stamina. Their workouts seldom exceed fifteen reps per exercise, which is why their massive muscles are "all show and no go" most of the time. At Spartan Race we often train in much higher rep ranges. Any time you exceed twenty to twenty-five consecutive repetitions on an exercise, you've entered the realm of what exercise physiologists call strength endurance, or what we in the Spartan world call stamina. Once you move out past thirty-five repetitions, you're out of the strength endurance range and into pure endurance.

Generally speaking, stamina is a product of your slow-twitch muscle fibers. While they've got staying power, they don't have the capacity to produce high levels of force. Force production is the realm of fast-twitch muscle fibers, which are strength oriented yet fatigue quickly. The benefits of one fiber type are the weak point of the other, which is why we need both fast and slow twitch.

Better muscular endurance results from several factors working together. First, when your muscle cells develop more mitochondria, which are the cellular power plants of the body, those muscles containing those cells can produce more energy aerobically. Along with more mitochondria come more myoglobin, aerobic enzymes, and capillaries to carry blood to your muscles. Muscular endurance training also prompts adaptation in the nervous system, enabling the body to recruit motor units in a more coordinated fashion. The more motor units that are recruited, the more forces that are produced. Also, the muscle fibers themselves change by increasing their cross-sectional area. A muscle's ability to produce force is positively correlated to its cross-sectional area.

Most important, muscular endurance training reaches the lactic acid threshold, that point at which the body can't supply muscles with oxygen at the rate they're using it. At this point, the body must supply the muscles with energy using the anaerobic (non-oxygen) energy system, which produces lactic acid in the muscles. If you've run up a hill before, you know what the lactic acid burn feels like. Muscular endurance training causes an increase in enzyme activity in the anaerobic energy system.

Muscular endurance training isn't normally associated with muscle growth, which is classically thought to be maximized in the eight-to-twelve-rep range. A study that was just being completed by Brad Schoenfeld, PhD, an assistant professor in exercise science at Leland College in the Bronx, New York, when I spoke to him suggests otherwise, though. "We looked at training for muscle endurance, which was basically twenty-five to thirty-five repetitions," he said. "We kept every variable the same except for the number of repetitions used. One group did eight to twelve; the other group did twenty-five to thirty. Over the eight weeks, we found no differences in muscle growth between the two protocols. However, we found that the lower-rep group received much better strength gains out of it, and the higher-rep group received much better muscle endurance out of it."

Most muscular endurance training will tax your core big time. "Core" isn't a synonym for abs — it's everything from the gluteal fold up to the bottom of the sternum. To use a car analogy, our core is, above all else, our transmission, which helps distribute and channel force through the lower body to the upper body in activities like throwing and climbing a wall. The core also stabilizes the body, working to resist unwanted motion in response to awkward loads. Notice men and women carrying a bag through the airport. Unless it's insanely heavy, I doubt they're totally bent over to the side. That's because their core is reflexively firing on the opposite side to even out the load.

Core training has become synonymous with crunches and sit-ups, but that's a limited view. In fact, I would argue that the body is not designed to do them for dozens upon dozens of reps. To a Spartan, core training ranges from explosive full-body exercises like burpees and spear throws to carrying heavy, awkward loads like our ancestors once did following their hunts. A stable load stays within the carrier's center of gravity. An unstable load, like a sandbag, forces an adjustment in the carrier's center of gravity. That requires more energy — meaning more calories burned — and it works muscles that otherwise wouldn't be used.

Spartan core training should be done outdoors whenever possible, because you can reap so many internal, emotional benefits in the presence of a virtually limitless selection of equipment. Carry rocks. Swap them for larger or smaller ones along the way. Do squats holding a log overhead, ending each set by throwing it off your shoulders explosively. The possibilities are endless.

Your resistance-training program should build stamina in the muscles that are going to do work during a race. Look at the event itself and try to develop the most endurance within those muscles that are going to be worked the hardest. The tricky part is that most of the body's musculature is worked hard by the various Spartan events. From there, you want to look at the planes of movement. Most of the activity in a Spartan Race is through the sagittal plane, which is the one that extends in front of you. If your goal is to accomplish that event, you would want to train mostly in that plane. Spend too much time moving laterally, and you're going to sacrifice some ability to do sagittal plane movements, because there's always an opportunity cost.

The other important thing is to train the energy systems that will help during a race or event. If you're doing, say, a marathon, you would want the aerobic endurance to run that duration. If you're looking to do more short bursts, the type of activity that might last ninety seconds, the fast glycolytic energy system will be called into action, and that can be developed through HIIT.

In a Spartan Race, sometimes you're jogging, sometimes you're sprinting, sometimes you're climbing a wall — and that's just the beginning of the demands imposed by the course. Like I said, the more specific your training becomes to race day, the better your transfer is going to be. Standing at the starting line with your fellow Spartans, you want the confidence that comes from knowing your strength, stamina, endurance, and athleticism have already been tested. If you've crushed most of your training but come up short in one key area, like stamina, all of your preparation may not be enough. It's a cliché, but in a Spartan Race, a person truly is only as strong as his or her weakest link.

I believe that the best way to develop unstoppable stamina is based on a certain style of training. Namely, there has been a lot of research produced in the last ten years that supports the effectiveness of HIIT for improving both anaerobic and aerobic fitness.

With stamina training, one of the most profound adaptations that takes place is the growth in the size and number of mitochondria. These little powerhouses of the cell are where oxygen is ultimately used to produce ATP, a molecule used to store and release energy. This is also where the body metabolizes fat as a fuel to make ATP. So if workouts can increase the concentration of mitochondria in muscle, the muscles will be able to produce greater quantities of energy aerobically, produce the energy at a faster rate, and be more effective at burning fat as a fuel.

All you really need for a stamina-building workout is to do numerous repetitions of a movement that requires you to exert a lot of force. It could be squats. It could be burpees. It could be pushups. What would not count? Running, because, although it's repetitious, it does not involve exerting a huge amount of force with every step. A jumping jack also is too light of a movement to merit muscular endurance status. As a rule, look for a movement you can't do constantly for more than two minutes without feeling fatigue in specific muscle groups.

Mountain climbers are a classic full-body exercise, and they develop full-body fitness as well, hitting your muscles and heart all at once. You'll probably go anaerobic (heavy breathing) if you do a handful. If you can pound them out while breathing normally, congratulations.

The burpee is the optimal dance between your body and gravity, and it will pay dividends for your entire body. No equipment needed. Hell, do your burpees wearing underwear first thing in the morning and you can have your daily workout taken care of before you brush your teeth. Do a bunch in a row and feel the ache all over your body as you start to suck wind. That will indicate that you are doing it right. Cardio plus strength equals your fitness foundation for Spartan Race. The burpee develops strength, power, muscle endurance, stamina, agility, mobility, and improves body composition. No major muscle group in the body is spared.

Planks are great for building real core strength, and they're harder than they look. When done properly, a plank can push your glutes and core to their limit. As the seconds tick, your whole body may shake and tremble. Good! Just don't let your form deteriorate. The world record holder held his plank for more than eighty minutes, so no complaining about your set.

Remember that strength is about more than simply picking up heavy shit and moving it from point A to point B, although our courses demand that capability. It's also about choosing to persevere through extreme adversity. It's a kind of faith, an unshakable belief that, despite the odds, you will make it; and that, once you've made it, the journey will be worth it. Our tagline is "You'll know at the finish line." Do we offer any proof? No. Do we calculate the odds of you knowing at the finish line? No. The tagline is merely an invitation into a different way of looking at the world, through the lens of Spartan Strength. People who come to view the world this way develop inner strength and an indomitable spirit.

3. ATHLETICISM

> "What a disgrace it is for a man to grow old without ever
> seeing the beauty and strength of which his body is capable."
>
> — SOCRATES

Athleticism isn't hard to recognize: Michael Jordan launching from the free-throw line and sailing through the air, tongue hanging out, in the 1988 slam dunk contest; Willie Mays sprinting back to the fence and making his no-look, over-the-shoulder catch in Game 1 of the 1954 World Series. However, athleticism isn't simply about sports. In the broadest terms, athleticism refers to skill-based movements that require balance, flexibility, and coordination. Raw strength and endurance aren't enough; they have to be coordinated and applied effectively. The good news is that, like strength and endurance, athleticism can be developed.

Movement is a skill. It takes years to develop the muscle memory—the neuromuscular connections in your nerves and brain —required to master a complex movement. It's akin to playing an instrument. Inborn talent helps, but you just can't walk up to a piano and start banging on the keys. How do you get to Carnegie Hall? Practice. The same is true of athletic movement. And, once developed, those skills will make you a much better athlete on the obstacle course, in other sports, and in life.

Few people know more about athleticism—in theory and in practice—than my friend Dan Edwardes, founder of Parkour Generations, the world's leading parkour organization. Not only has Dan starred in ads for Nike and MTV, but, with a degree from Cambridge University, he has the brains to back it up. Dan is a microcosm of what athleticism requires: a neuromuscular connection between brains and brawn.

"Think of a time in your life," Dan told me, "when you moved at a fairly constant and high intensity, day in and day out, and likely very rarely encountered any overuse injuries. There's a good chance that time was your childhood, when you were playing all day long, running, jumping, climbing, fighting, crawling, dropping, and didn't give a moment's thought to correct form or good alignment."

We often forget that play isn't pointless but has a critical biological function: skill development. It's why lion cubs play at pouncing on prey, and why baby gazelles play at eluding predators. It's why human kids not only engage in raw physical play but also go crazy for toys (object play) and make-believe (social play). Human survival long depended on physical athleticism, tool use, and social interactions — so kids instinctively practice these skills.

"Now, there's also a good chance you've forgotten how to move effortlessly through years of inactivity," Dan continued, "or even through deconstructing your movement so much in overprogrammed, rigid gym methodologies that isolate one part of your body while neglecting other parts — which typically leads to the weakest part of the chain eventually snapping."

Even the strongest, most well-conditioned professional athletes run into this issue. Sports have become increasingly specialized and present a huge risk of repetitive stress injuries such as tennis elbow, golfer's elbow, and runner's knee. Entirely new surgical procedures have been developed specifically to repair the broken bodies of professional athletes, such as Tommy John surgery (Tommy John was a pitcher for the Dodgers). Weekend warriors face some of the same risks as professional athletes, particularly at the beginning of their training, since they have yet to redevelop good form and healthy movement patterns.

Dan's advice: "Move well, then move fast and well."

"Your body knows how to move well with regard to its own unique anatomy, you just have to get out of your own way and allow it to do so. Move holistically, avoid too much time on isolated, specialized exercises, and find a way to restore that playful, joyful, childlike mover within you. Run, jump, crawl, and climb, and it will begin to come back, and you'll find your natural movement patterns reestablishing themselves. This isn't to say you should stop utilizing supplementary exercises for strength, power, and coordination, but do remember these are only supplementary to and supportive of the overriding function of the human body, which is to move through and adapt to variable terrain."

With that in mind, let's start with some of the key elements of athleticism.

Posture

Posture is the foundation of human athleticism. I feel like a grand-mother lecturing people on their posture, but Granny was right: stop slouching. When your skeleton is misaligned, your body will instinctively compensate — ever tried to walk with a normal gait on a sprained ankle? Even when we are pain-free, most of us are walking around with less acute versions of sprained ankles, thrown-out backs, and tweaked shoulders. And the body subconsciously compensates in subtle ways that can come back to haunt you as mysterious injuries.

Crucial to good posture is maintaining a healthy spine. Through an alternating system of bony vertebrae and shock absorbing discs, the human spine manages to be both highly flexible and superstrong. Once those discs rupture, though, your spine will never be the same. And you know what puts immense pressure on them? Slouching. Hunching over at a desk. Sitting. Which is why I want you to stand up straight. Start using a standing desk. Buy one, or just put a crate or small table on top of your existing desk. When you do sit, remember to stand up from time to time. Spartans aren't hunched over unless they're lacing 'em up for a race.

Stretching

Athleticism requires flexibility and range of motion. I highly recommend stretching, because it improves your range of motion for nearly every exercise known to man, supports good posture by lengthening muscles that have shortened over time, reduces your risk of suffering muscle pulls during training and races, allows for faster recovery post-workout, and is an effective method to reduce stress.

Yet stretching remains the bastard stepchild of the fitness world. Everyone knows weights and cardio produce visible or measurable results, yet the feeling persists that stretching is kind of a waste of time, that it's not really *doing* anything. In reality, the benefits of a stretch can be immediate. Every trainer on the planet understands an exercise called the squat, and many trainers watch a client perform that to gauge their depth, which indicates a client's flexibility in the hips, glutes, hamstrings, and ankles. The trainer is looking to see where the movement stops. Well, if that client does one good hip flexor stretch, he or she could see major improvement.

Stretching is so much more than "static stretching"—the familiar quad, Achilles, and toe-touch stretching that so many do before jogging. Stretching covers a spectrum of techniques: static, dynamic, ballistic, trigger point, pre-event, pre-activity, post-activity, off-season, in season, preparatory, restorative, getting stretching by a specialist, massage, and one of my favorite activities: yoga. Unfortunately, many people still do static stretching before a workout. This has the opposite effect of what's intended. Static stretching will actually shut down function, perhaps even setting the table for an injury during your workout. Instead, you want your stretching before your workout to be movement based. For a detailed treatment of mobility from an expert, pick up a copy of *Becoming a Supple Leopard* by Kelly Starrett.

Balancing

Balance and proprioception (awareness of body position) are also put to the test in any Spartan Race, whether it's by running down a narrow trail or hopping from foot to foot across a series of logs. If someone gets injured in a Spartan Race, it's usually because they've fallen. Balance is a skill that we are intuitively trained in when young, but then stop practicing it. How many gyms have equipment to practice your balance? Everything is flat and bolted into place.

In the gymnasiums of ancient Greece, athletes trained barefoot, which strengthened their feet and lower legs and assisted with balance even when they were on solid ground. Do the same by spending as much time as possible barefoot (even though you can keep shoes on during your workouts). Walking barefoot in deep sand is a tremendous foot workout, one that will strengthen the muscles that help you balance. Also, place a log or wooden board on the ground and walk along it, or use the curb on any street. As you progress, practice carrying things while you're balancing or doing exercises like lunges on your plank.

Crawling

We all crawled before we walked, and in doing so we all set in motion a cascade of profound, lifelong adaptations. The spine was subjected to gravity in a new position, and gravity leads to the infant's musculoskeletal system becoming far more active than before. Perhaps most profoundly, the shape that the spine assumes in crawling begins to create the curves of our lower back (lumbar) and upper back (thoracic) that we'll have for a lifetime. Interestingly, many experts agree that infants who skip crawling or are rushed into walking are at a greater risk for back pain later in life.

Somehow folks lose this innately human skill of crawling as they grow up. But we make racers crawl under barbed wire in our races. When someone crawls, their shoulders are forced to grow much stronger in order to support the torso. The torso — or core — is then forced to engage not only to stabilize the spine but also to act as a point of "transmission" for opposing upper and lower body limbs to work together synergistically. This is key. The core is designed to not only connect but equalize and balance opposing forces. Try to sprint as fast as possible without moving your arms. The body is one piece and needs to be trained and developed as such, so what better tool could we possibly use than the "exercise" that taught us all these skills in the first place?

Climbing, Reaching, and Swinging

Climbing is an impulse humans share with other primates. And what do many children instinctively do when they get to a playground, or find themselves at the base of a tree? They climb. It's natural and fun. I'm not saying you need to compete with kids (or monkeys) in this area, but you should be able to lift yourself out of life's precarious situations. If you were drowning and all you had to do was climb a rope to survive, could you do it?

Every Spartan Race includes climbing of walls, ropes, and terrain. Climbing requires grip strength, upper-body pulling strength, lower-body pushing strength, and full-body balance and coordination. To practice climbing, start by hanging from a pull-up bar and performing pull-ups and their variations. Make it harder by hanging or doing pull-ups from a towel draped over a bar. Climb a tree or go rock climbing. See if any gyms in your area have a setup to actually practice a rope climb.

Reaching and swinging are tactical builds on the skills and strengths developed in crawling and climbing. Since swinging poses a higher risk for injury than other movements, one should first master simple hangs, pull-ups, and climbs before transitions are added. There's nothing worse than missing a swing or reach and stressing an arm unfit to support your body weight. Once you can hang for two minutes, progressively practice reaching side to side and in front of you. Go to a playground and use the monkey bars. And if you live near a set of rings, like those at the Santa Monica Pier, you can start to practice swings and how to effectively harness your body's own momentum.

Jumping

Jumping is all about power and explosive energy to quickly move either horizontally or vertically. Jumping uses our fast-twitch muscle fibers, but our fast-twitch capacity is quickly lost when it's not trained and it deteriorates naturally with age. Arguably the most important form of exercise for the elderly is plyometrics, explosive movements exerting maximal force — which is the only way to slow the deterioration of fast-twitch muscles that makes it difficult for old folks to rise from their chairs. Jumping should be practiced on both one and two legs through long and vertical jumps. At a Spartan Race, the key to climbing an eight-foot wall or conquering other obstacles often comes down to how good of a jump you get onto it. So get explosive — it might save you thirty burpees.

Lifting

Lifting is another critical skill, and it begins with posture. When descending to ground level, it's biomechanically natural to a human to squat. From the bottom of a squat we should be able to not only lift, but also garden, fish, cook, play, relax, and even go to the bathroom. Another natural method to lift something from the ground is to "hinge" at the hips, using slightly less knees and keeping our hips higher above the ground. Performed properly, this deadlift-style movement harnesses the power of our glutes instead of relying on weaker back and arm muscles. However, most sedentary people lose the ability to hinge at the hips and instead bend from the lower back, which loads their lumbar spine — the typical way to injure the back when lifting heavy boxes or furniture.

So in addition to avoiding a lot of sitting, to get good at lifting you need to 1) do a lot of squats, and 2) work on your hip hinge. At the race you'll need to flip tractor tires and pick up Atlas stones, both of which will need a quality hip hinge to perform safely and effectively. A simple exercise is to lie on your back, knees bent, feet flat on the floor. Pick up your hips into a bridge, leaving your head, shoulders, and feet on the floor. Hold for twenty seconds, then relax and repeat for three to four minutes. To practice your actual hip hinge, stand with your back about twelve inches from a wall. Hold a yardstick (or similarly straight implement) against the length of your spine, holding one end at your tailbone and the other end at your neck. Make sure the yardstick remains in contact with your head, mid-back, and tailbone as you slowly "push" your tailbone back toward the wall without consciously bending your knees. You should feel this in the hamstrings. Once you can hinge, go hiking and pick up random heavy stones and logs. Yoga helps too, as does a good trainer who can gradually teach you how to deadlift properly.

Carrying

The most ancient form of "weight training" was probably carrying a child. In the wild, hunters had to carry an animal carcass; gatherers had to carry an armful of tubers. It only got harder: in 480 B.C., the 300 Spartans marched more than 220 miles to Thermopylae, each carrying up to 100 pounds of armor, weapons, and supplies. And, outside of modern gyms, carrying has often been an asymmetrical activity, since most natural loads have an uneven distribution of weight and irregular holds.

Spartan Races require participants to carry heavy buckets,

sandbags, and stones — and you'll get plenty of practice in the 30-Day Plan. Lots of ordinary chores are opportunities to practice too. You can carry as many bags of groceries as possible in one trip, carry your child or dog for part of a long hike, or help friends and family move. You can also take the stairs when carrying things, or pick up random rocks or logs on a hike. But remember, the most critical part of a carry is picking up the weight and putting it back down — so always use proper squat or deadlift form.

Pulling and Dragging

Most Spartan Races include a tractor pull, tire drag, or hoisting heavy weights with a rope. Pulling and dragging large, heavy objects across rugged terrain requires head-to-toe efficiency and it will stress muscles that you didn't realize existed. For training, tie a rope or chain to a cinderblock and drag it through some rocky terrain. While usually not the most physically difficult obstacle, it can require more mental toughness than most people anticipate. When you can't do it anymore, just imagine Ernest Shackleton's stranded expedition dragging their supplies across Antarctica, or the Lewis and Clark team porting their equipment across the western United States in the early 1800s.

Throwing

Humans have used projectile weapons for tens of thousands of years, which played a key role in hunting and tribal warfare. Evidence suggests that humans evolved specific adaptations for throwing ability, a skill that everyone should practice. Not simply an isolated arm motion, a powerful throw transmits the force of the entire body, through the core, into a projectile.

In a Spartan Race, everyone approaches the spear throw with trepidation — they have one shot, it's an unfamiliar movement, and they don't want to do thirty burpees. I don't actually recommend trying to practice spear throwing — it's more exciting as a novel test of athleticism. Just throw around a football, baseball, or play darts with some buddies. And practice your burpees, just in case.

Swimming

Unlike in a triathlon, you won't be swimming long distances during a Spartan Race, but swimming is a great way to prepare for it. Swimming improves breathing, cardiovascular fitness, and muscle mass, and it requires balance and coordination. It's a low-impact activity that can be performed well into old age. One of the heroes of Spartan Race is Jack LaLanne, who swam for an hour a day until he passed away at age ninety-six. Go and do likewise.

No matter how you train your athleticism, always remember the advice of Dan Edwardes: "Move well, then move fast and well." And practice.

4. RECOVERY

> "If a man insisted always on being serious, and never allowed himself a bit of fun and relaxation, he would go mad or become unstable without knowing it."
>
> — HERODOTUS

A Spartan Race is designed to subject the human body and mind to stress. At first glance, breaking people down might even seem purposeful, like it's the whole point of our races. So the more stress, the better, right? Not necessarily.

As Spartans, we do stress our bodies and challenge our minds, but we don't do it continuously or mindlessly. We know from research and personal experience that a body eventually breaks down if it never stops or downshifts. So we train hard and attack life every day while bearing in mind certain realities. We're very aware that intense training requires equally intense recovery and recuperation. We stress our bodies and challenge our minds with epic tasks, but we don't allow trivial things to snowball into major stress episodes. We like the feeling of being sore, and we expect some bumps and bruises out on the course, but we don't seek to injure ourselves, because that would be stupid. We always live to race another day.

So we take rest days, mindful that the brain and body both need sufficient amounts of rest. You will find these days listed as "active restoration" in the 30-Day Plan. Finding that balance in life is something each person must do for themselves.

If you think stress is some vague force, preoccupying your mind but divorced from your body, the following story should make you reconsider. Back in 1833, a Native American suffered a gunshot to his abdomen, a wound that left his gut tissues exposed. He survived, and, much to the surprise of those tending to him, his gut tissues were always bright pink — that is, unless he grew angry or otherwise stressed. At those moments, his gut tissues suddenly became white.

Fast-forward to 1936, when endocrinologist Hans Selye coined the term "stress" to explain the ill health effects of ongoing external threats to an organism. He arrived at this notion without ever having to navigate voice prompts when calling his bank, seeing his ex-girlfriend on Facebook having fun with someone else, or learning from a health website that every little ache is a symptom of a heart attack. Selye noticed that if mice were traumatized long enough, they all developed stomach ulcers. The experiment sounds a little perverse, but it did make a significant contribution to the emerging science of mental health. Stress is real.

When we experience stress today, our bodies handle it in a way that has a lot to do with the evolution and survival of our species. In prehistoric times, you wouldn't sit in a cave having your nerves jangled by handheld devices going ping-ping-ping-ping every few seconds. Stress came in forms such as a wild beast trying to eat you, which made you run for your life. And so the internal hormonal response to stress has been coded into our DNA as preparation to defend us against an imminent threat to our survival.

Times have changed. In the most recent 1 percent of human history, stress hasn't always been that need for a sudden burst of adrenaline. Today, stress, if we let it, can become constant or at the very least chronic. It comes at us from every direction: crying children, traffic jams, work difficulties, financial woes, and marital problems (in that order). It turns many people into a ball of stress that can be very difficult to untangle.

We like to think humans are finely tuned organisms. This organ does this, this system does that, and so on, everything operating in its own neat little compartment or sphere of influence. In reality, however, we are a chaotic, interconnected mess of highly sensitized pathways, with almost nothing operating on an independent circuit. Everything depends on something else, and if you stress one system, it will spill over to affect many systems, even if it takes years to manifest itself. Your diet, exercise, thoughts, and feelings are all going to affect your performance, mood, digestion, reproductive ability, attention, and everything in between. This is why things like rest and meditation are as essential to becoming a Spartan as doing burpees.

You need to develop a set of practices and rituals that reliably allow you to relax. For example, practice deep breathing several times each day. Take a series of deep breaths, followed by drawn-out yet forceful exhalations. If you know you need a good night's sleep, go for a long hike with weight on your back and *sweat*, then finish up with a cold plunge or ice-cold shower — you'll sleep so well. Wake up to another cold plunge or shower. Meditate or pray for at least five minutes per day, more if possible. Take a yoga class or two each week. Spend time laughing with your friends. Look for ways to incorporate more meaningful communal interactions in your life, and engage in some sort of spiritual practice.

Rest and stress reduction are also an essential part of avoiding injuries.

My philosophy is to train hard but to stop short of injury. That might sound obvious, but an injury can manifest itself in many ways. There's the acute pain experienced after a muscle pull, a disc injury in the spine, or some other injury. There's also soreness from tissue damage that sneaks up on you in the days after a workout or race. How to distinguish between acceptable and unacceptable levels of discomfort?

The burn you feel in a muscle while training reflects the buildup of lactic acid and other metabolites. That pain is transitory.

Another normal feeling of discomfort comes from delayed-onset muscle soreness (DOMS), which reflects small injuries to muscle tissues. While DOMS might reduce strength in the short term, and make it hard to walk up a stairwell at work the next day, it doesn't reflect any long-term damage.

The challenge is differentiating DOMS from more serious problems, such as tendinitis (i.e., inflammation of a tendon) or a muscle strain. Here, duration of discomfort is key. DOMS typically becomes noticeable twenty-four hours after a workout or race, peaks at around forty-eight hours, and dissipates after seventy-two hours. If the pain is worsening rather than improving after three days, or you reach a point where the limb or body part can't perform routine tasks, stop your training and see a doctor. By the time most people seek medical help, they're beyond DOMS and suffering from an overuse or overtraining injury, such as tendinitis or tenosynovitis, an inflammation of a tendon and its protective sheath. Treatment can range from rest and the application of heat or cold to immobilizing the affected area.

Luckily there's a way to overcome the good hurt, and it all comes down to things like stretching, foam rolling, and even massage. Foam rolling is a very effective way to massage your muscles yourself. Always drink lots of water too. This helps to flush out all the lactic acid and keeps your muscles hydrated. Go sweat in a sauna for twenty minutes. Or take a cold plunge. And of course, get plenty of sleep.

During sleep, much of the body's most important restoration occurs. When did you last sleep without interruption for eight hours? That's how much shut-eye the National Sleep Foundation suggests the adult human body needs to function at its best.

Let's start with sleep's effect on the brain. Studies have found that sleep strengthens memories and even practice skills that are learned while awake. "If you are trying to learn something, whether it's physical or mental, you learn it to a certain point with practice," says David Rapoport, MD, an associate professor at NYU Langone Medical Center. "But something happens while you sleep that helps you to learn it better."

Sleep also helps to restructure, sort, and organize memories. Researchers at Harvard University and Boston College found that people somehow strengthen the emotional components of a memory during sleep. In turn, this may actually help spur the creative process. A well-rested mind is also an ordered mind. Studies have shown that only one night of sleep deprivation can make someone feel as if they are driving under the influence of too much alcohol.

Sufficient sleep also lengthens your attention span. If you were reading this now on short sleep, you probably would struggle to follow what I'm writing. Quick fixes such as sugar, caffeine, and other stimulants don't last; moreover, they may lead to addictions in some cases. In contrast, sleep is a good, free resource available to everyone.

The connection between sleep and health may have a lot to do with inflammation. One of the most accurate inflammation measures is a blood marker called C-reactive protein, and researchers have found it elevated in those who sleep six hours or fewer on average. This is unhealthy, because inflammation is linked to hypertension, heart disease, stroke, type 2 diabetes, and arthritis, among other serious health issues.

Lack of sleep during the workweek can't be made up with binge sleeping on the weekend either. "If you sleep more on the weekends, you aren't sleeping enough in the week," says Dr. Rapoport. "It's all about finding a balance."

Research has found a direct connection between quality of sleep and weight loss. University of Chicago researchers discovered that dieters lost more weight when they were well rested. "Sleep and metabolism are controlled by the same sectors of the brain,"

Dr. Rapoport says. "When you are sleepy, certain hormones go up in your blood. It's those same hormones that drive appetite." Think back to those times when you had insomnia and raided the fridge. How healthy were your food selections?

Lack of sleep can also impair your athleticism. A Stanford University study found that college football players who tried to sleep at least ten hours a night for seven to eight weeks improved their average sprint times, had less daytime fatigue, and improved overall stamina. The results of this study echo previous findings concerning tennis players and swimmers.

Keep in mind that two nights before your event is the most important sleep night, not the night before. For example, the Thursday night before a Saturday race is your "money night" to get some great sleep. Avoid eating during the couple hours before you go to bed, and stop drinking anything at least three hours beforehand, so you don't wake up to pee. And don't drink anything besides water. (And the day before the race, go out for twenty-five minutes and re-create at a slower pace what you will be doing in the race.)

I'll be the first to admit that with my busy schedule running Spartan Race, I don't always get as much sleep as I'm recommending here. This is a rare case of "Do as I say, not as I do." Life often gets in the way, but it's worth striving to sleep more. Stress is real — so don't think of rest and relaxation as "doing nothing," but rather as doing something critically important.

5. NUTRITION

"Let medicine be thy food and let food be thy medicine."

— HIPPOCRATES

Hippocrates was an ancient Greek physician now known as the "father of Western medicine." He wrote one of the most famous texts in medicine, the original Hippocratic oath, in which ancient physicians would swear to ethical conduct. Today, doctors recite a modernized version when they graduate from medical school and utter the famous words "first do no harm." When Hippocrates said that food was a form of medicine, he wasn't suggesting that you could cure cancer with an apple; what he meant was that eating the right foods might assist in preventing numerous diseases.

But what are the "right" foods? People have been debating this point since Hippocrates passed away in 371 B.C., and each new controversy seems to launch a new lunacy. First, it's a low-fat craze, then a low-carb fad, then a high-protein revolution, and on and on. This "diet du jour" mentality drives me nuts, because diets don't permanently address the way you eat. The goal is to teach you to feed yourself for the rest of your life, not stop after dropping a few pounds. As with your training, changing the way you eat needs to be a lifestyle change, not merely some fad diet that won't last. You need to begin eating nutritious foods instead of junk, and you need to eat that way from here on out.

Everyone has an opinion about food — and in *my* opinion, everyone is making it way more complicated than it needs to be. Spartans didn't obsess over calories, measure the exact macronutrient ratio of their diet, get on a scale, and take pictures in the mirror every day. They didn't make extravagant or indulgent dishes. They ate a simple diet, but a nutritious one — whole foods, grown and raised in the local countryside, prepared and cooked in traditional ways. And when Spartan soldiers marched to war, I'm sure they made do with whatever food was available. The rest took care of itself.

All that said, most people today didn't grow up with a wholesome diet, might have a broken (or nonexistent) relationship to food, or are trying to address specific health conditions or goals such as weight loss or performance. Plus, ancient Spartans never had to face the nearly unlimited choices in a grocery store. So, modern times may call for more attention paid to our dietary habits. But the end goal remains the same: a simple and sane relationship to food.

As my coauthor, John Durant, points out in his book, *The Paleo Manifesto,* it makes sense to start way, way back: the Paleolithic. For over a million years, our ancestors were nomadic foragers who scavenged, hunted, and gathered wild foods. Hunter-gatherers might stay in one place for a week or two and use up the available resources before moving on. Over the course of a year, they might exploit twenty to thirty plant foods as staples and ten to fifteen species of animals, fish, or both. They were omnivores and ate quite a broad and opportunistic diet. Their dietary options were limited less by explicit rules than by the foods available prior to agriculture. About 10,000 years ago, the Agricultural Revolution dramatically altered the human diet, which became heavily concentrated in domesticated cereal grains and, in some cultures, dairy from domesticated animals. A few hundred years ago, the Industrial Revolution shifted the typical human diet to processed foods, such as sugar, refined flour, and vegetable oils. And that, unfortunately, has contributed to a massive obesity epidemic.

Obesity is one of the leading causes of preventable death in the United States. In most cases, more frequent workouts won't fix the problem completely. It's a cliché, but you truly can't out-train a bad diet. What's more, an unhealthy diet is dangerous even if it *doesn't* result in weight gain. The term "skinny fat" refers to having a normal body weight while still having the metabolic markers of the obese, such as hypertension, high levels of the bad kind of LDL cholesterol, and high blood glucose. Not everyone wants or needs to lose weight; weight maintenance and healthy weight gain are worthy objectives for some people, and excellent dietary habits play a role in achieving these goals as well.

According to diet expert Fred Bisci, PhD, what you *don't* eat is often more important than what you *do* eat. When we spoke with Dr. Bisci, he hammered home one point above all others: eliminate all overly processed foods. Skip the soda, pizza, and candy. Food manufacturers and even nice restaurants often load their dressings, soups, and sauces with sugar and sodium. Salt doesn't have to be eliminated from the diet, but don't add it in everything you eat. Only after you have cut out junk food and started eating whole food should you worry about the ratios of carbs, fats, and proteins. If you're eating lunch at McDonald's, a chia salad at dinner isn't going to make you healthy, even if it were raw, organic, and grown in the next-door neighbor's yard.

To become Spartan Fit you must replace industrially processed foods with whole ones: fresh fruits, vegetables, meats, seafood, eggs, grass-fed poultry, and certain healthful oils. The change alone will skyrocket the nutrient density of your diet. Whichever diet you subscribe to, consume foods in a state as close to nature as possible. Real foods grow; they are not created in a lab. Real foods have names like "apple." Real foods don't have a nutritional label. If what you're eating has ingredients you can't even pronounce, you shouldn't be eating it. When you find labels that are indecipherable, put the item back on the shelf. If you can't figure out what it is, most likely your body won't know what to do with it either. If there's a TV commercial for it, don't eat it. Real foods generally don't have a big ad budget.

Many have asked . . . do Spartans drink? Hah. If you've ever hung out with us during a race weekend, you know some of us do. I don't, and I think many people use studies showing the positive effects of moderate alcohol intake to justify excessive alcohol intake. The studies may define "moderate" as no more than one or two drinks per day, but I suggest no more than one or two drinks per week! Excessive drinking offers no health benefits and is associated with cirrhosis of the liver, hypertension, stroke, and type 2 diabetes. As for water, if you're eating a healthy diet and avoiding large amounts of alcohol and coffee, your own sense of thirst should become a good guide to water intake.

Personally, I like the simplicity of Michael Pollan's advice: "Eat food. Mostly plants. Not too much." It seems to equally enrage vegan purists for including meat and paleo purists for favoring plants and including some grains and dairy. Here's a radical notion: maybe both approaches can contribute to the food movement in different ways. I fall on the plant-based side of the spectrum, but I know a lot of modern Spartans eat paleo too. Maybe we can work together. The plant eaters can lead the charge on getting people to eat their fruits and veggies, and the animal eaters can support pasture-based animals and wild food systems. I realize that's far too radically reasonable, and I'll probably be excommunicated by the vegan *and* paleo purists. So be it.

Rather than tell you exactly how to eat, I'm going to give you a few Spartan nutrition principles to guide your eating instead of planning out every meal down to the turnip.

Spartan Nutrition Principle #1: Avoid Processed Foods.

First, do no harm. Highly processed foods — soda, candy, cookies, fast food, hot dogs, sugary cereals — aren't just devoid of much nutritional value; they are harmful. Industrial processing not only adds extra sugars and sodium, but it also can add trans-fats, hormones, antibiotics, and a host of chemicals that may not be healthful over the long run. Highly processed foods come with many risks and few benefits, and they can be addictive. Better to just avoid them.

Spartan Nutrition Principle #2: Eat Whole Foods, Especially Fruits and Vegetables.

Eat food that your great-grandmother would recognize as food. Most people already have meat in their diets, and so I emphasize including way more plants. Raw fruits and vegetables will give you the energy and micronutrients you need. You also need protein and healthy fats, but plant foods provide energy and phytochemicals that are essential for good health. Unfortunately, the intake of fruits and vegetables around the world falls well below recommended levels.

Spartan Nutrition Principle #3: Eat Nothing Sometimes.

It's not the end of the world to miss a meal. I often train without food or water just to acclimate my body to harsher conditions. Plus, there's a wealth of scientific evidence that the occasional fast — say, sixteen to twenty-four hours — is beneficial. It's probably no accident that so many cultural traditions around the world include some type of fasting.

Spartan Nutrition Principle #4: Adapt.

I don't like dependence on any diet, including a "perfect" one. Hunter-gatherers adapted to their surroundings, and Spartans made do with what was available. Humans are opportunistic omnivores, and that means we have more dietary flexibility than probably any other species on the planet. Unless someone has a full-fledged allergy or autoimmune condition, a little bit of this or that isn't going to kill them. Plus, everyone has different dietary needs depending on genetics, gut biome, lifestyle, and goals, so it's foolish to think that one precise way of eating is ideal for everyone on the planet. Develop resilience and adapt.

And that's pretty much it. For those who want specific guidance on getting started on a healthier path, there is a set of recipes starting on page 206. Just don't expect anything complicated or gourmet; we selected simple recipes for staple foods — the Spartan way. And if you feel like complaining, just be glad you aren't eating black broth — pig's blood, salt, and vinegar — in the Spartan mess halls.

6. MIND

> "In life our first job is this, to divide and distinguish things into two categories: externals I cannot control, but the choices I make with regard to them I do control. When will I find good and bad? In me, in my choices."
>
> — EPICTETUS

Seneca was a Stoic philosopher who decried the corrupting influence of wealth and leisure. He was also perhaps the wealthiest man in ancient Rome, amassing a fortune estimated at three hundred million *sestertii*, large enough to place himself in the top tier of today's billionaires.

Was Seneca a hypocrite? How could someone so rich, who built his fortune as advisor to the infamously ruthless emperor Nero, be an exemplar of simplicity and frugality?

But Seneca wasn't against wealth, per se — he was against *dependence* on wealth. And he used a series of mental exercises to ensure that he didn't become habituated to luxury. Today, the average American takes for granted luxuries that would have been the envy of Rome: grapes in winter, an automobile, air conditioning. And so many of us have become dependent on little luxuries: a morning latte, a smartphone, or Wi-Fi. Perhaps Seneca's wisdom is more relevant than ever.

One of Seneca's habits was to spend a few days each month living in poverty. He would travel around Rome or the countryside as an indigent, perhaps a shipwrecked traveler, and then return to one of his opulent estates full of newfound appreciation. His discourse is worth quoting at length:

I am so firmly determined, however, to test the constancy of your mind that, drawing from the teachings of great men, I shall give you also a lesson: Set aside a certain number of days, during which you shall be content with the scantiest and cheapest fare, with coarse and rough dress, saying to yourself the while: "Is this the condition that I feared?" It is precisely in times of immunity from care that the soul should toughen itself beforehand for occasions of greater stress, and it is while Fortune is kind that it should fortify itself against her violence. In days of peace the soldier performs manoeuvres, throws up earthworks with no enemy in sight, and wearies himself by gratuitous toil, in order that he may be equal to unavoidable toil. If you would not have a man flinch when the crisis comes, train him before it comes. Such is the course which those men I have followed who, in their imitation of poverty, have every month come almost to want, that they might never recoil from what they had so often rehearsed.

. . . Let the pallet be a real one, and the coarse cloak; let the bread be hard and grimy. Endure all this for three or four days at a time, sometimes for more, so that it may be a test of yourself instead of a mere hobby. Then, I assure you . . . you will leap for joy when filled with a pennyworth of food, and you will understand that a man's peace of mind does not depend upon Fortune; for, even when angry she grants enough for our needs.

Seneca would *practice misfortune* every month. What a concept: to practice misfortune in the same way that a soldier trains for battle. To challenge the mind with mental obstacles in the same way we challenge the body with physical obstacles.

I've gotten the chance to meet a lot of cool people — authors and athletes, entrepreneurs and soldiers — and interview them on the Spartan Up! podcast. These are people who have to perform at a high level in extreme situations, from the boardroom to the battlefield, where maintaining a sound mind is essential. They all have their own tips and tricks, routines and rituals, habits and practices that help them maintain a sound mind in our increasingly frenetic world.

One of the most common themes has been to start every day on the right foot. It's important to find a routine — a set of rituals — that allows you to set a positive and productive mindset for each day. The key part is finding actions that you can control, rather than becoming dependent on external factors, such as the news, that can throw your day into a tailspin if they don't happen according to plan.

General William H. McRaven, former Navy admiral and head of U.S. Special Operations Command, gave me a simple suggestion: "The first thing you should do each morning is make your bed, so you have already accomplished something when your day starts." As it turns out, there's a fair bit of research behind his recommendation. Gretchen Rubin, best-selling author of *The Happiness Project,* found that making your bed was the most common response when she asked people what made them happy. Another survey of 68,000 people by Hunch.com found that 71 percent of people who make their bed consider themselves happy. People who didn't make their bed? Sixty-two percent considered themselves *un*happy. Make your bed! How simple and effective.

When reflecting back, almost everyone will agree that their happiest times were during or immediately following the pursuit — the work, challenge, or action that got them to that moment. Happiness isn't something that just falls from the sky, and it's not something that we should expect or demand. We "earn" happiness through our thoughts and actions. Happiness comes easy through hard work.

Another good part of a morning routine is some type of meditation, prayer, or motivational mantra. It's okay if it's the exact same thing every morning — the author Steven Pressfield recites the invocation of the Muse from Homer's *Iliad* before he sits down to write.

Just as important as what to do in the morning can be what *not* to do. Tim Ferriss tries not to check email in the morning until he's had time to work on his most important priority for the day. Email will not only overwhelm you, it will also distract you from your most important long-term priorities.

And is it really worth checking the news? Nassim Taleb follows the idea of a "news fast" and regularly avoids news on the web, TV, or in newspapers. The daily news is worse than white noise; it's consistently negative — not necessarily because the world is getting worse, but because the media know that negative stories capture our attention more than positive stories. If something really important happens, Taleb hears about it from other people in his life. Unplug from the outrage and hype machine.

Many people say that between kids and work, they don't have time to exercise in the morning, but that's the wrong way to look at it. First, the idea of "having time" is a passive way to look at life, as if it's out of your control. Take control: make time. For most people, that means going to sleep earlier. You have to prioritize things that are important to you. And even a cold shower is better than nothing. Stretching is easy and I stretch everywhere. I was recently in an airport and found some Spartans in the same terminal wearing shirts after a race. I convinced all of them to do three hundred burpees with me and stretch while we sat waiting for our plane. There is always time.

Among people who do exercise regularly, there's another common mental deficit: becoming a gym rat. I spoke about it with my friend Zach Even-Esh, founder of the Underground Strength Gym.

"I used to be a slave to the gym," Zach said, "and was so closed-minded that I could see no other way to exercise unless I was sitting on machines lifting under perfect conditions or walking on the treadmill to nowhere. My friends would invite me mountain biking and I would reply, 'Not today, it's leg day at the gym.' They laughed and told me that mountain biking *is* leg day! Not only was I missing out on quality time with loved ones, but I was also hurting myself with the lack of variety. I finally hit a wall after my second knee surgery, an ACL repair.

"I canceled my gym membership, went to Home Depot, and bought a sledgehammer and wheelbarrow for the backyard. I filled up the wheelbarrow with rocks and pushed it up and down my driveway. An old tree had to be taken down, so we cut it into five-foot logs and used them to carry, squat, and lunge. It was a much more meaningful way to exercise that went far beyond how big my muscles looked. And it was fun: I rode my bike to the local playground and used the monkey bars. I rebuilt my leg strength to the point where I could push my truck across empty parking lots. I felt alive again.

"Now I view all forms of movement as training, no longer a slave to a specific routine. I go surfing and swim; play tennis with my kids; hike, bike and run on trails and streets; and I'm open and willing to anything else that is movement and play. The gym is everywhere we look, it's all around us."

Learn to view the world as your gym. The ancient Greek gymnasiums were outdoors, and Spartan Races are out in nature. Get out there.

The 30-Day Plan — and this entire book — are sprinkled with suggestions to test your mind in addition to your body. Much of it will probably seem really hard and you won't want to do it. In my conversation with Steven Pressfield, I asked him how he overcomes the heavy feeling of not wanting to do something.

"Well, my thoughts on this came from being a writer," Pressfield said. "And as you know, there's a million people who think they can write, right? But when you feed paper into a typewriter or face a blank screen, all of a sudden, everything changes. And you really become aware that coming off that blank page is this force — a negative force, just like to take a cold shower or to go for runs. This 'No, no, no, no,' and it comes up with a million reasons why you shouldn't do that. And that voice in your head begins undermining your self-confidence: 'Who are you to think you can start a business? Who are you? You had an idea for a race? Well, who's gonna come to this race? You? Why should I listen to you?' That is a voice of resistance."

I hear that voice every day. Every goddamn day.

"And as a writer, for years that voice would steamroll me and defeat me. And finally, I just realized it's not me — it's not *me* that's thinking that thought, it's just this force called resistance with a capital *R*."

I *love* this concept. Names are powerful — call it by its name: it's not resistance, it's Resistance.

Pressfield pointed out a subtle but important effect of this change in perspective. "It takes away the judgment. It takes away that terrible burden of 'There's something wrong with me,' or 'I'm sick.' Instead, it's just 'Oh, I was thinking wrong. I just had a wrong attitude.'"

It might be inside of you, but it's not *you*.

"So, that changed my whole life," Pressfield continued. "When I woke up in the morning, I said to myself, 'I expect this negative force.' I expect this thing, this enemy — the aliens, the shark in *Jaws*, whatever it is. It's relentless, it will never give up. And I just thought, well, each morning — just like you — I have to defeat this thing. There's a dragon, I gotta slay it. And so, you evolve certain techniques — like you've evolved with your races — that will give you energy, give you strength, give you perseverance. Because you have to defeat it. There's no way to fake your way around it."

Resistance never goes away. When you recognize it pushing back on you, name it, and externalize it, something amazing happens. Not only can you learn to overcome it but you can also let it guide you to what you should be doing. As Marcus Aurelius said, "The impediment to action advances action. What stands in the way becomes the way."

7. CODE

"Not life, but good life, is to be chiefly valued."

— SOCRATES

Over time, you may find that you start to think and act differently than other people, that you adhere to a different outlook on life — a code that guides you philosophically, ethically, and morally. It may seem silly until the day it becomes real to you, but it's very real to me. As the training of ancient Spartan warriors allowed them to fight as a unified phalanx, so this code unites the Spartan community.

THE SPARTAN CODE

Spartans push their mind and body to its limits.

Spartans master their emotions.

Spartans learn continuously.

Spartans give generously.

Spartans lead.

Spartans stand up for their beliefs, no matter the cost.

Spartans know their flaws as well as their strengths.

Spartans prove themselves through actions, not words.

Spartans live every day as if it were their last.

6

THE 30-DAY PLAN TO SPARTAN FIT

"A goal without a plan is just a wish."

— ANTOINE DE SAINT-EXUPÉRY

THIS 30-DAY WORKOUT plan will prepare you to tackle a Spartan Sprint and more. The workout plan is a lot like a Spartan Race: fun, challenging, varied, and full of surprises. Your body won't know what's coming from one workout to the next, and that's exactly the way I want it. However, before you start any new exercise and diet regime, you should consult with your doctor. This workout plan is hard — really hard — but imagine the feeling of accomplishment when you finish it.

All that said, have fun! Exercise is not a chore for me. It is part of who I am. Find joy in suffering. Team up with a friend for these workouts, or meet as a group. Blast your favorite playlist. Run in a scenic park. Celebrate your commitment and hard work each day.

I hope that this 30-day period sparks — or continues — a lifetime of movement.

Chapter Index
- FAQ: Getting Started
- Beginner's Program
- Prep Checklist
- Day 0: Test Day
- The 30-Day Plan
- How to Perform the Exercises

FAQ: GETTING STARTED

Below are some frequently asked questions for getting started.

Why thirty days, instead of two weeks, months, or years?
There is nothing magical about thirty days, except that it's enough time to achieve noticeable results and prepare you to complete a Spartan Race.

What benefits can I expect to see?
This plan builds all the core attributes of fitness we've already discussed: endurance, strength, and athleticism. It will benefit your performance in any sport, whether you're a serious athlete or a weekend warrior. While training, you will probably drop some pounds and add some muscle. But think of that as a byproduct of training rather than the main goal. Besides the physical change, this training will also benefit other aspects of your life.

Be aware of how the training positively impacts you. How do you feel on the days you train? Are you less stressed, more energetic? More clear-headed? Happier? Do you have more fuel in the tank, powering you to take on the inevitable challenges of the day, and make the most of the opportunities before you? If you realize how the training serves you on a daily basis, you will be more likely to stick with it.

Where should I work out? Do I need to join a gym?
All the workouts should be done outside; don't let a little bad weather deter you. But the most important thing is to adapt to wherever you find yourself — whether a hotel gym, a local park, a beach, or your backyard. Just get it done.

Do I need to buy a lot of equipment?
No. I encourage you to find equipment available in your surround-ings (rocks, logs, parks, playgrounds, etc.) or build it yourself. There's a lot you can do with stone, wood, rope, and mud. I in-cluded a prep checklist to help you get started.

What if I don't know how to perform an exercise?
In this guide, there is less handholding and spoon-feeding than there is with most fitness plans, but everything you need is in this chapter. I included "Day 0" to learn the standard warm-up, perform a baseline test of your fitness, and practice cooling down. Days 1 to 30 list the workout of the day and instructions. Later in the chap-ter there is an exercise index with an explanation of each move-ment and photos to illustrate. Training videos can also be found at Spartan.com.

Why do you use the metric system for distances?
I want obstacle racing to be recognized as an Olympic sport one day (see chapter 8). Therefore, Spartan Race is leading the charge to meet standards for Olympic events, all of which use the metric system. You will begin to see us use the metric system (meters, ki-lometers) in addition to more familiar yards and miles. One meter is just longer than a yard, 400 meters is about a quarter mile, and 1,600 meters is about one mile.

Should I eat before, during, or after the workouts?
I want you to do these workouts on an empty stomach to take ad-vantage of training in a glycogen-depleted state, which will fire up your internal fat-burning machinery. Carry some carbohydrate with you on longer workouts just in case you begin to experience

symptoms of low blood sugar (extreme muscle weakness, light-headedness, nausea, etc.).

What if the workouts are too hard?

You will be training hard here, but not so hard that you'll feel the need to bail. I would encourage you to follow the workouts exactly as designed. I've collaborated with several exercise physiologists to design them in a way that should tax your body without overwhelming it. If you do less than we suggest, you might not move with enough intensity to grow and adapt. If you do more than we suggest, you might wind up overtraining.

If you are truly incapable of lifting a weight, have an existing injury, or your body is telling you that you're getting injured, then scale the workout appropriately—but scale it to a level that is still harder than you think you can do. Then do it.

Seriously, what if I am right off the couch?

If you are significantly overweight, spend a month doing the Beginner's Program in the next section. When you can complete the Test Day without risk of injury, begin the 30-Day Plan.

What if the workouts are too easy?

Ha, I'm glad you asked. If you are a seasoned athlete who has completed a Spartan Race and trains regularly, feel free to incorporate some of our "Spartan Elite Modes" listed in chapter 7. These modes are designed to test your mental fortitude as much as your physical conditioning and will turn any ordinary workout into an extraordinary one.

What should I do on rest days? What is "active restoration"?

Active restoration days aren't workout days, per se—but I don't want you sitting on the sofa eating Cheetos with your buddies either. I want you to keep your limbs moving, your blood flowing, and your lungs and heart pumping, albeit not as hard as they would be during a Spartan workout or race. So, on your active restoration days, still do something to make yourself better. Some of my favorite active restoration techniques include ice baths and cold showers — which I take every day — meditation, yoga, or other forms of stretching, and foam rolling or other tissue-manipulation techniques. You don't even have to get fancy with infrared saunas and flotation tanks. Just go for a walk with friends, a loved one, or even your dog.

Being healthy is about more than exercise, which is why I also encourage you to use rest days to improve other parts of your lifestyle: mental health, stress relief techniques, sleep quality, food, and personal relationships. When your next training day rolls around, you'll be ready to dominate your workout.

BEGINNER'S PROGRAM

If you are significantly overweight, I strongly recommend focusing on your diet and making some lifestyle changes before beginning the 30-Day Plan. You need to get to a place where you can comfortably complete the Test Day (dead hang, burpees, running) without risk of injury. Remember, don't worry about the finish line — the first step is getting to the starting line.

- Follow the Spartan nutrition principles in chapter 5:
  - Avoid processed foods.
  - Eat whole foods, especially fruits and vegetables.
  - Eat nothing sometimes (fast).
  - Adapt.
- Cook the recipes in the back of this book.
- Don't eat for 4 hours before bed. Drink nothing aside from water.
- Get more sun during the day and more sleep at night.
- Take the stairs.
- Complete the following each day, even if you have to spread it out:
  - 1 hour of walking outside
  - 10 high pushup holds (hold the top of a pushup position for as long as possible)
  - 30 squats (or 30 couch stand-ups — sit on couch then stand up)

- Bonus: Bikram yoga once per week.

PREP CHECKLIST

Pick your spots

- ☐ Scenic trails: _____
- ☐ Hill, steep ascent (or stairs): _____
- ☐ Pull-up bar: _____
- ☐ Playground (monkey bars and obstacles): _____
- ☐ Yoga studio: _____
- ☐ Gym (optional): _____

Get the gear

- ☐ Running shoes (a pair you don't mind getting dirty)
- ☐ Stopwatch or timer (small and portable)
- ☐ Bucket (five-gallon plastic bucket)
- ☐ Sandbag (standard is 50 lb. for women, 70 lb. for men)
- ☐ Stone, large (standard is 80 lb. for women, 115 lb. for men)
- ☐ Stone, medium (something you can carry for a long time)
- ☐ Log, long (to use as a balance beam)
- ☐ Log, short (about 2 ft. long)
- ☐ Jump rope

Practice the movements

- ☐ Review the exercise index and try unfamiliar movements.
- ☐ Visit Spartan.com for video demos.

Make it social and commit

- ☐ Find one or more friends who will suffer with you.
- ☐ Pick an important reason why you're training.
  #WhyIRace: _____
- ☐ Commit publicly by posting on social media. Tag Spartan
  Race with #ChallengeAccepted.

DAY 0: TEST DAY

> "The best preparation for good work tomorrow
> is to do good work today."
>
> — ELBERT HUBBARD

1. Warm-up

This warm-up is designed to increase your heart rate, prepare the major joints and muscle groups for movement, and practice contra-lateral movements (skipping, crawling). Perform at a relaxed pace that leaves you warm and just starting to sweat. Complete before every workout.

- 10 ankle circles and wrist circles (5 in each direction)
- 5 minutes jog, row, bike, or jump rope
- 2 rounds of:
  - 30m skipping
  - 10m bear crawl
  - 10m reverse bear crawl
  - 10m walking lunges
  - 10 squats

2. Workout

Complete these three fitness tests in sequence as if they were a mini–Spartan Race.

- Dead Hang Test — hang from a bar for as long as possible, palms out. Record time.
- Burpee Test — do as many burpees as possible in 5 minutes with race form. Record reps.

- Distance Test — run (or walk) as far as you can in 30 minutes. Record distance.

	HELL NO	SO SO	AROO!
Dead Hang Test	< 30 sec.	30–60 sec.	> 90 sec.
Burpee Test	< 40 reps	40–65 reps	> 65 reps
Distance Test	< 5 km	5–7 km	> 7 km
	(< 3.1 miles)	(3.1–4.3 miles)	(>4.3 miles)

3. Cool-down

Finish each workout with a few minutes of static stretching or light yoga. Your muscle tissue is warm and elastic at that point, so it's the ideal time to increase your flexibility.

NOTES

_____

_____

_____

_____

_____

_____

_____

_____

_____

DAY 1: DOWN AND UP

> "The Spartans do not ask how many the enemy are,
> but where they are."

— KING AGIS II OF SPARTA

Instructions:

Find a 100m stretch of grass. Mark off every 25m (1 meter = 3.28 feet, or one normal stride). Aim for a seamless transition between all movements. If you can no longer do pushups, do them from your knees. *Every workout includes the Day 0 warm-up and cool-down.*

5 rounds for time:

- 10 pushups
- 25m army crawl
- 25m bear crawl
- 25m sprint
- 25m skipping
- 10 squat jumps (max height)
- jog 100m back to start

NOTES

_____

_____

_____

_____

_____

_____

_____

_____

DAY 2: BUCKET LADDER

> "We do not have to become heroes overnight.
> Just a step at a time."
>
> — ELEANOR ROOSEVELT

Instructions:

Find a 400m loop. Prepare to fill a bucket (5-gallon, plastic) with rocks, dirt, sand, or water after each lap. Carry the bucket with your arms, not a shoulder or handle.

For time:

- 400m run
- 400m bucket carry (25% full)
- 400m bucket carry (50% full)
- 400m bucket carry (75% full)
- 400m bucket carry (100% full)
- 400m run

NOTES

_____

_____

_____

_____

_____

_____

_____

_____

_____

DAY 3: EASY 60

> "Endurance is one of the most difficult disciplines, but it is to the one who endures that the final victory comes."
> — BUDDHA

Instructions:

Complete this workout on a beautiful trail or scenic route, not a treadmill. If you can't run for the full time, hike until you can run again. Maintain an easy pace (below your lactic threshold).

- 60 minutes run (easy pace)
- 60 burpees

NOTES

_____

_____

_____

_____

_____

_____

_____

_____

_____

_____

_____

_____

_____

DAY 4: ACTIVE RESTORATION

"The sky is not the limit . . . I am."

— T. F. HODGE

Suggestions:

- Take a yoga class. Hot yoga is a good way to relax tight muscles.
- Take a cold shower for at least 20 seconds.
- Play with your kids (no matter how old they are).
- Fast for 16 hours, including overnight (water or tea only).
- Call a friend or relative whom you haven't seen recently.
- Get rid of any ambient electronic light in your bedroom.

NOTES

_____

_____

_____

_____

_____

_____

_____

_____

_____

_____

_____

_____

_____

_____

DAY 5: TEXAS HOLD 'EM

> "We are what we repeatedly do. Excellence, then, is not an act but a habit."
>
> — ARISTOTLE

Instructions:

Find a pull-up bar, tree branch, or anything you can hang from. If you can't dead hang continuously for the required time, then rest and count cumulative hang time. If you can't do strict pull-ups, then jump into the pull-up.

3 rounds of:

- 2 minutes dead hang
- 10 pushups (hold each rep for 5 seconds at the top)
- 10 squats (hold each rep for 5 seconds at the bottom)
- 10 pull-ups (hold each rep for 5 seconds at the top)
- 10 standing broad jumps (hold the landing, don't stumble past)

NOTES

_____

_____

_____

_____

_____

_____

_____

_____

_____

DAY 6: FAST 20

> "Do not consider painful what is good for you."
> — EURIPIDES

Instructions:

Perform this workout at a speed that feels somewhat hard to max effort. If you can't maintain a fast pace, then alternate between slow and fast every minute rather than moving at a consistently moderate pace.

- 20 minutes run, bike, swim, or row (somewhat hard to max effort)

NOTES

_____

_____

_____

_____

_____

_____

_____

_____

_____

_____

_____

_____

_____

_____

DAY 7: BURPEES FIVE WAYS

> "If you bite off more than you can chew, keep chewing."
>
> — JOE DE SENA

Instructions:

Learn to love the burpee. Find a pull-up bar, tree branch, or anything you can hang from. Drape a towel over it for the dead hang (though you don't have to use the towel for the burpee pull-ups).

- 1 minute towel-over-bar dead hang
- 5 rounds for time:
  - 5 hand-release burpees (at bottom of pushup, lift hands off the ground)
  - 5 burpee pull-ups (jump into a pull-up)
  - 5 strict pushup burpees (perfect plank pushups)
  - 5 burpee broad jumps (jump forward as far as you can)
  - 5 burpees (race standard)
- 1 minute towel-over-bar dead hang

NOTES

_____

_____

_____

_____

_____

_____

_____

_____

DAY 8: OLYMPUS CARRY

> "The impediment to action advances action. What stands in the way becomes the way."
>
> — MARCUS AURELIUS

Instructions:

Go to a hill with a short, steep ascent and find a rock or log. (Stairs with a medicine ball or weights are acceptable.) Alter how you carry the object as needed, but don't put it down.

Repeat for 40 minutes:
- Brisk walk up the hill carrying a rock or log
- Easy jog down the hill carrying the rock or log

NOTES

_____

_____

_____

_____

_____

_____

_____

_____

_____

_____

_____

_____

DAY 9: ACTIVE RESTORATION

"Adopt the pace of nature: her secret is patience."

— RALPH WALDO EMERSON

Suggestions:

- Make your bed in the morning.
- Find a long log and walk across it to practice your balance.
- Buy a fruit or vegetable that you've never tried before. Try it.
- Go through your old clothes and give them away to charity.
- Laugh. Watch a comedy. Go see improv or stand-up.
- Meditate or pray for 10 minutes.

NOTES

_____

_____

_____

_____

_____

_____

_____

_____

_____

_____

_____

_____

_____

_____

_____

DAY 10: HERO — HANG TIME

"Those who can bear all can dare all."

— LUC DE CLAPIERS, MARQUIS DE VAUVENARGUES

Instructions:

This Hero workout is over once you accumulate 10 minutes of hang time on the bar. Each time you come off the bar, there is a 5-burpee penalty. Your final score is the total time it takes you to accumulate 10 minutes of hang time and complete the penalty burpees — thus, a perfect score for unbroken hang time is 10 minutes. You will need two modes of timekeeping: one for on-bar time (a stopwatch) and one for total time (a phone or watch).

For time:

- 10 minutes dead hang (cumulative time on the bar)
- 5 burpees each time you come off the bar

NOTES

_____

_____

_____

_____

_____

_____

_____

_____

_____

_____

_____

DAY 11: SPORT

> "Lack of activity destroys the good condition of every human being, while movement and methodical physical exercise save it and preserve it."
>
> — PLATO

Instructions:
Play a sport you enjoy for at least 1 hour. Or try a new one.

Suggestions:
- Basketball, touch football, soccer, hockey, volleyball, tennis
- Water sports: swimming, paddleboarding, surfing, kayaking
- Martial arts: MMA, wrestling, jujitsu, judo, karate
- Rock climbing, Ultimate Frisbee, gymnastics, skateboarding
- Winter sports: skiing, snowboarding, cross-country skiing

NOTES

_____

_____

_____

_____

_____

_____

_____

_____

_____

_____

_____

DAY 12: BURPEE BUCKET CRAWL

"That which does not kill us makes us stronger."

— FRIEDRICH NIETZSCHE

Instructions:

Find a 400m loop. Fill a bucket with rocks, dirt, sand, or water. Carry the bucket with your arms, not on a shoulder or by a handle.

5 rounds for time:
- 10 burpees
- 400m bucket carry (50% full)
- 25m army crawl

NOTES

_____

_____

_____

_____

_____

_____

_____

_____

_____

_____

_____

_____

_____

_____

_____

DAY 13: EASY 75

> "I hated every minute of training, but I said, 'Don't quit. Suffer now and live the rest of your life as a champion.'"
>
> — MUHAMMAD ALI

Instructions:

Complete this workout on a beautiful trail or scenic route, not a treadmill. If you can't run for the full time, hike until you can run again. Maintain an easy pace (below your lactic threshold).

- 75 minutes run (easy pace)
- 75 burpees

NOTES

_____

_____

_____

_____

_____

_____

_____

_____

_____

_____

_____

_____

_____

_____

_____

DAY 14: ACTIVE RESTORATION

> "Enjoy present pleasures in such a way as not to injure future ones."
>
> — SENECA

Suggestions:

- Build a cold plunge, and take one.
- Spend 30 minutes on a foam roller.
- Practice doing handstands and somersaults.
- Build a standing desk. (A crate or footstool on a desk will do.)
- Feast day — you're halfway there! Eat a big meal with others.
- Leave your cell phone outside your bedroom at night.

NOTES

_____

_____

_____

_____

_____

_____

_____

_____

_____

_____

_____

_____

_____

_____

_____

DAY 15: SANDMAN

> "Don't ask for a light load, but rather ask for a strong back."
> — UNKNOWN

Instructions:

You must travel 400m, one sandbag throw at a time. The sandbag chest throws and underhand throws allow you to advance — so make the most of them — but the slams and sit-ups must be performed in place. Men use a 70-lb. sandbag, women use a 50-lb. sandbag.

400m for time:

- 10 sandbag chest throws (advance the distance thrown)
- 10 sandbag underhand throws (advance the distance thrown)
- 10 sandbag slams (in place)
- 30 sit-ups (in place)

NOTES

_____
_____
_____
_____
_____
_____
_____
_____
_____
_____

DAY 16: FAST 30

"Sweat cleanses from the inside. It comes from a place showers will never reach."

— DR. GEORGE SHEEHAN

Instructions:

Perform this workout at a speed that feels somewhat hard to max effort. If you can't maintain a fast pace, then alternate between slow and fast every minute rather than moving at a consistently moderate pace.

- 30 minutes run, bike, swim, or row (somewhat hard to max effort)

NOTES

_____

_____

_____

_____

_____

_____

_____

_____

_____

_____

_____

_____

_____

_____

DAY 17: LITTLE STONEHENGE

> "The block of granite which was an obstacle in the pathway
> of the weak, became a steppingstone in the pathway of
> the strong."
>
> — THOMAS CARLYLE

Instructions:

Use a heavy stone. Race standard is 115 lb. for men, 80 lb. for women. A kettlebell works too, but using a difficult grip is part of the idea. Remember, deadlifts are a leg exercise, not a back exercise. And for the Atlas carry, use a proper squat to pick up and set down the stone.

5 rounds for time:
- 25 stone deadlifts
- 25m Atlas carry
- 25m sprint (no stone)
- 25m bear crawl (no stone)

NOTES

_____

_____

_____

_____

_____

_____

_____

_____

_____

DAY 18: OLYMPUS CARRY SPRINTS

"Then imitate the action of the tiger; stiffen the sinews, summon up the blood."

— SHAKESPEARE

Instructions:

Go to a hill with a short, steep ascent and find a rock or log. (Stairs with a medicine ball or weights are acceptable.) Alter how you carry the object as needed. Count rounds.

Repeat for 40 minutes:

- Sprint to the top of a hill empty-handed. Run down.
- Walk back up carrying a rock/log. Walk down with it.

NOTES

_____

_____

_____

_____

_____

_____

_____

_____

_____

_____

_____

_____

_____

DAY 19: ACTIVE RESTORATION

> "Time eases all things."
> — SOPHOCLES

Suggestions:

- Fast for 18 hours, including overnight (water or tea only).
- Do deep-breathing exercises.
- Play with your pets.
- Look up the closest farmers' market and go. Meet a farmer.
- Read a book for one hour.
- Flirt with your spouse or partner. He or she has noticed your progress. Make a move.

NOTES

_____

_____

_____

_____

_____

_____

_____

_____

_____

_____

_____

_____

_____

_____

DAY 20: HERO — HELEN OF SPARTA

> "Nothing happens to any man that he is not formed by nature to bear."
>
> — MARCUS AURELIUS

Instructions:

Helen of Sparta was abducted and carried off to Troy, sparking the decade-long Trojan War. After the Greeks proved victorious, she finally returned to Sparta. Carry the sandbag on your shoulders during the runs. Race standard is a 70-lb. sandbag for men, 50-lb. sandbag for women, but scale as necessary.

For time:
- 3km sandbag run (1.9 miles)
- 100 burpees
- 3km sandbag run (1.9 miles)

NOTES

_____

_____

_____

_____

_____

_____

_____

_____

_____

DAY 21: SPORT

> "The more you sweat in peace, the less you bleed in war."
> — GENERAL GEORGE PATTON

Instructions:

Play a sport you enjoy for at least 1 hour. Or try a new one.

Suggestions:

- Basketball, touch football, soccer, hockey, volleyball, tennis
- Water sports: swimming, paddleboarding, surfing, kayaking
- Martial arts: MMA, wrestling, jujitsu, judo, karate
- Rock climbing, Ultimate Frisbee, gymnastics, skateboarding
- Winter sports: skiing, snowboarding, cross-country skiing

NOTES

_____
_____
_____
_____
_____
_____
_____
_____
_____
_____
_____
_____
_____

DAY 22: TEST DAY

"Nearly all men can stand adversity, but if you want to test a man's character, give him power."

— ABRAHAM LINCOLN

Instructions:

Complete these three fitness tests in sequence as if they were a mini–Spartan Race. Compare results to Day 0.

- Dead Hang Test — hang from a bar for as long as possible, palms out. Record time.
- Burpee Test — do as many burpees as possible in 5 minutes using race form. Record reps.
- Distance Test — run (or walk) as far as you can in 30 minutes. Record distance.

NOTES

_____

_____

_____

_____

_____

_____

_____

_____

_____

_____

_____

_____

DAY 23: EASY 90

> "We must all either wear out or rust out, every one of us. My choice is to wear out."
>
> — THEODORE ROOSEVELT

Instructions:

Complete this workout on a beautiful trail or scenic route, not a treadmill. If you can't run for the full time, hike until you can run again. Maintain an easy pace (below your lactic threshold).

- 90 minutes run (easy pace)
- 90 burpees

NOTES

_____
_____
_____
_____
_____
_____
_____
_____
_____
_____
_____
_____
_____
_____

DAY 24: ACTIVE RESTORATION

> "Instead of using medicine, rather, fast a day."
>
> — PLUTARCH

Suggestions:

- Fast for 24 hours, including overnight (water or tea only).
- Volunteer in your community.
- Play a game with your friends.
- Use a sauna or steam room.
- Write a thank-you note.
- Call someone you had a falling-out with.

NOTES

_____

_____

_____

_____

_____

_____

_____

_____

_____

_____

_____

_____

_____

_____

_____

_____

DAY 25: DOUBLE SANDMAN

> "Be sure you put your feet in the right place, then stand firm."
> — ABRAHAM LINCOLN

Instructions:

You must travel 800m, one sandbag throw at a time. The sandbag chest throws and underhand throws allow you to advance — so make the most of them — but the slams and sit-ups must be performed in place. Men use a 70-lb. sandbag, women use a 50-lb. sandbag.

800m for time:

- 10 sandbag chest throws (advance the distance thrown)
- 10 sandbag underhand throws (advance the distance thrown)
- 10 sandbag slams (in place)
- 30 sit-ups (in place)

NOTES

DAY 26: FAST 40

> "Whether you think you can, or you think you can't —
> you're right."
>
> — HENRY FORD

Instructions:

Perform this workout at a speed that feels somewhat hard to max effort. If you can't maintain a fast pace, then alternate between slow and fast every minute rather than moving at a consistently moderate pace.

- 40 minutes run, bike, swim, or row (somewhat hard to max effort)

NOTES

_____

_____

_____

_____

_____

_____

_____

_____

_____

_____

_____

_____

_____

DAY 27: BIG STONEHENGE

> "Strength and growth come only through continuous effort and struggle."
>
> — NAPOLEON HILL

Instructions:
Use a heavy stone. Race standard is 115 lb. for men, 80 lb. for women. A kettlebell works too, but using a difficult grip is part of the idea. Remember, deadlifts are a leg exercise, not a back exercise. And for the Atlas carry, use a proper squat to pick up and set down the stone.

5 rounds for time:
- 50 stone deadlifts
- 50m Atlas carry
- 50m sprint (no stone)
- 50m bear crawl (no stone)

NOTES

_____

_____

_____

_____

_____

_____

_____

_____

_____

_____

DAY 28: OLYMPUS CARRY SPRINTS

> "A man's health can be judged by which he takes two at a time — pills or stairs."
>
> — JOAN WELSH

Instructions:

Go to a hill with a short, steep ascent and find a rock or log. (Stairs with a medicine ball or weights are acceptable.) Alter how you carry the object as needed. Count rounds. Compare with Day 15.

Repeat for 40 minutes:

- Sprint to the top of a hill empty-handed. Run down.
- Walk back up carrying a rock/log. Walk down with it.

NOTES

_____

_____

_____

_____

_____

_____

_____

_____

_____

_____

_____

_____

_____

DAY 29: ACTIVE RESTORATION

> "The general who wins the battle makes many calculations in his temple before the battle is fought. The general who loses makes but few calculations beforehand."
>
> — SUN TZU

Suggestions:

- Meditate or pray for 10 minutes.
- Don't log onto social media for 24 hours.
- Give someone a small gift for no reason.
- Try acupuncture, massage, cryotherapy, or a float tank.
- Cook a meal with someone. Try a new recipe.
- Have great sex with your spouse or partner.

NOTES

_____

_____

_____

_____

_____

_____

_____

_____

_____

_____

_____

_____

_____

DAY 30: HERO — THE HOT GATES

"Molon labe."

— KING LEONIDAS OF SPARTA

Instructions:

The Spartans marched more than 220 miles to Thermopylae, then fought the Persians for 3 days. This workout begins with a long run, followed by 3 rounds of punishment — 300 reps, one for each Spartan. Male standard is a 70-lb. sandbag and full bucket; female is a 50-lb. sandbag and 75% full bucket. For time. *Novices should scale down this extremely difficult workout.*

- 10km run (6.2 miles)
- 5 minutes rest

3 rounds of:
- 100 burpees
- 100m sandbag walking lunges (out)
- 100m army crawl (back)
- 100m bucket carry (out)
- 5 minutes rest

NOTES

_____

_____

_____

_____

_____

_____

HOW TO PERFORM THE EXERCISES

Below is an exercise index, followed by descriptions and photos. You can also find video demonstrations, as well as additional exercises and workouts, at Spartan.com.

Burpees
- Standard Race Burpee
- Burpee Broad Jump
- Burpee Pull-Up
- Hand-Release Burpee
- Strict Pushup Burpee

Carries and Lifts
- Stone Deadlift
- Atlas Carry
- Bucket Carry

Circles
- Ankle Circles
- Wrist Circles

Crawls
- Army Crawl
- Bear Crawl
- Reverse Bear Crawl

Dead Hangs
- Dead Hang
- Towel-over-Bar Dead Hang

Lunges
- Walking Lunge
- Sandbag Walking Lunge

Pull-Up

Pushup

Sandbags
- Sandbag Chest Throw
- Sandbag Run
- Sandbag Slam
- Sandbag Underhand Throw
- Sandbag Walking Lunge

Sit-Up

Skipping

Sprint

Squats
- Squat
- Squat Jump

Standing Broad Jump

BURPEES
Standard Race Burpee

1. Begin in a standing position. Keeping your hips high, reach down and place your hands on the ground in front of you.
2. Kick your legs straight out behind you and assume the top of a pushup position.
3. Lower your torso to the ground like a pushup and touch the ground with your chest.
4. Push off the ground.
5. Jump both feet forward between your hands, hips high.
6. Return to a standing position. jump straight up in the air, and clap your hands overhead.

Note: Race burpees should be done as fast as possible in a fluid motion. Judges will check for four points: 1) chest-to-deck during pushup, 2) full hip extension while standing, 3) feet leaving the ground, and 4) hands raised above ears during jump. To avoid injury, always maintain a neutral spine and activated core.

Burpee Broad Jump

Perform a standard race burpee, but instead of jumping straight up in the air, jump forward as far as possible.

Burpee Pull-Up

Perform a standard race burpee underneath a pull-up bar. When you jump up in the air, grab the bar (instead of clapping your hands) and use your momentum to complete a pull-up.

Hand-Release Burpee

Perform a standard race burpee, but at the bottom of the pushup release your hands from the ground and extend (*cont. on page 152*)

Standard Race Burpee

Step 1

Step 2

Step 3

Step 4

Step 5

Step 6

them outward like airplane wings. Your weight will momentarily rest on your chest and toes. After full arm extension, return your hands to the ground beneath your shoulders, complete the pushup, and finish the burpee.

Strict Pushup Burpee

Instead of the rhythmic or fluid motion of the standard race burpee, perform a burpee with the utmost control and precision. Ensure a perfect plank is achieved and a strict pushup is executed. Absolutely no worming or flopping.

CARRIES AND LIFTS

Stone Deadlift

1. Stand over the stone with it placed between your feet.
2. Descend from the hips and knees while maintaining a tall spine and proud chest.
3. Wrap the stone in both arms, pulling it tight to your torso.
4. Stand using your hips and legs, not your back. Achieve a full upright position.
5. Using proper squat technique, gently return the stone to the ground.

Note: It's very easy to overload your spine during the pickup and put-down. Keep your core engaged and spine in the upright and neutral position at all times.

Atlas Carry

1. Perform a stone deadlift to the upright position.
2. Hold the stone tight to your torso and walk the required distance.
3. Using proper squat technique, gently return the stone to the ground.

Note: It's very easy to overload your spine during the pickup and put-down. Keep your core engaged and spine in the upright and neutral position at all times.

Bucket Carry

1. Fill a 5-gallon plastic bucket with gravel, sand, or water.
2. Stand with the bucket between your feet (similar to the stone deadlift and Atlas carry).
3. Descend from the hips and knees while maintaining a tall spine and proud chest.
4. Wrap the bucket in both arms, pulling it tight to your torso.
5. Stand using your hips and legs, not your back. Achieve a full, upright position.
6. Hold the bucket tight to your torso with your arms wrapped around it or hold the bucket from the bottom with extended arms.
7. Walk the required distance.

8. Using proper squat technique, gently return the bucket to the ground.

Note: At the race, buckets cannot be carried on the shoulders (but logs can).

CIRCLES
Ankle Circles

1. Balance on one leg.
2. Extend the opposite leg and rotate the ankle. To go beyond circles, "write" the first ten letters of the alphabet with your foot by moving your ankle.
3. Repeat for the opposite leg.

Wrist Circles

1. Place your hands in front of you with palms together, fingers interlocked, and elbows together below your wrists and hands.
2. Rotate your wrists in large circles.
3. Repeat in the opposite direction.

CRAWLS
Army Crawl

1. Lie on the ground on your stomach.
2. Support your upper torso by placing your elbows directly beneath your shoulders. Position your knees outside your hips, with the inner side of your knees on the ground. The torso, elbows, and knees should now all be in contact with the ground.

3. Crawl forward by alternating the opposing arm and leg, moving in unison.

Bear Crawl

1. Get on your hands and knees the way a baby crawls (hands beneath shoulders, knees beneath hips, and a flat spine). Then, lift your knees an inch off the ground.
2. Step forward with one arm and the opposing leg at the same time.
3. Repeat with the opposite arm and opposing leg.

Note: Maintain a long, neutral neck position throughout the movement.

Reverse Bear Crawl

Start in the same position as a bear crawl, but move backward instead of forward.

DEAD HANGS

Dead Hang

1. Hang from a pull-up bar with your feet off the floor.
2. Maintain a rigid torso, an active scapula, and tight grip. Avoid allowing the shoulders to elevate toward the ears.
3. Hold this position for the prescribed duration.

Towel-over-Bar Dead Hang

Drape an old towel over a bar and grip the towel instead of the bar during the dead hang. Works for pull-ups too.

LUNGES

Walking Lunge

1. Stand with your feet shoulder-width apart. Maintain a tall chest, eyes straight ahead.
2. Take a large, but natural, step forward with your left foot.
3. Bend both legs as you lower your right knee toward the ground as low as is comfortable, with the goal of just grazing the ground with your right knee.

4. Push with your left leg and lift your right knee, stepping forward to a standing position.
5. Repeat with the opposite leg.

Sandbag Walking Lunge

Perform a walking lunge with a sandbag on one of your shoulders. Switch the sandbag to the opposite shoulder as appropriate to work both sides equally.

PULL-UP

1. Hang from a pull-up bar with palms facing out (palms facing in is a chin-up).
2. Maintain a rigid torso, an active scapula, and tight grip. Avoid allowing the shoulders to elevate toward the ears.
3. Pull your body upward until your chin is over the bar.
4. Descend to the starting position with control.

Note: It's important to practice pull-ups, since the palms-out grip is more versatile than a chin-up in real-life situations (wall, cliff, branch).

PUSHUP

1. Assume a pushup position: rigid body parallel to the ground supported by your toes and fully extended arms, hands beneath your shoulders.
2. Lower your torso to the ground and graze it with your chest.
3. Push off the ground and back into the starting position.

Note: Maintain control and a rigid torso throughout movement. Make sure your elbows do not flare out beyond 45 degrees from your sides.

SANDBAGS

Sandbag Chest Throw

1. Stand tall holding the sandbag at chest height, arms bent with elbows by your sides.
2. Forcefully extend your arms and throw the sandbag forward.
3. Move forward and pick up the sandbag, then repeat as prescribed.

Sandbag Run

1. Stand tall with a sandbag on either shoulder or across your back.
2. Run for the prescribed time or distance, alternating shoulders as necessary.

Sandbag Slam

1. Stand tall holding the sandbag at chest height, arms bent with elbows by your sides.
2. Lift the sandbag directly overhead with arms fully extended.
3. As forcefully as possible, slam the sandbag to the ground directly in front of you, allowing yourself to descend into a slight squat as you do so.

4. Pick up the sandbag and repeat as prescribed.

Sandbag Underhand Throw

1. Stand tall with the sandbag between your feet.
2. Descend into a semi-squat (hips and knees, not back) and pick up the sandbag with both hands and arms fully extended.
3. Swing the sandbag beneath your legs once or twice, then forcefully toss it forward. Your back should remain firm and straight, and you should hinge at the waist and knees to generate power.
4. Move forward to the sandbag and repeat for the prescribed repetitions or distance.

Sandbag Walking Lunge

Perform a walking lunge with a sandbag on one of your shoulders. Switch the sandbag to the opposite shoulder as appropriate to work both sides equally.

SIT-UP

1. Lie on your back with your knees bent and feet flat on the floor.
2. Maintaining a tall chest and an upward gaze, push your feet into the floor as you "sit up" from the hips and torso.
3. Gently return to the starting position.

SKIPPING

You remember how to skip, don't you?

1. Stand tall with a rigid torso.
2. Bound forward off one foot, forcefully flexing the knee upward and ensuring the opposing arm reciprocates with a similar upward and forward motion.
3. Immediately repeat on the opposing side and continue for the prescribed distance.

SPRINT

1. Run as fast as possible maintaining a slight forward lean.
2. Alternatively, pretend a bear is chasing you and proceed accordingly.

Note: Increase your efficiency by keeping the arms bent around 90 degrees and pumping the elbows back and forward with each stride.

SQUATS
Squat

1. Stand strong with feet shoulder-width apart and turned slightly outward.
2. "Sit" back, descending the hips until the thighs are just below parallel to the ground.

3. Contract your glutes and return to the starting position.

Note: Maintain a tall chest, eyes forward, and heels on the floor throughout the squat. Do not let your knees cave inward during any part of the movement.

Squat Jump

1. Stand strong with feet shoulder-width apart and turned slightly outward.
2. Quickly descend into a quarter-squat position and forcefully project your body into a vertical jump.
3. Land softly, descending into a squat position to absorb the force.
4. Continue immediately into the next squat jump.

Note: Maintain a tall chest, eyes forward, and heels on the floor throughout the squat. Do not let your knees cave inward during any part of the movement.

STANDING BROAD JUMP

1. Stand tall, then raise your arms overhead.
2. In a fluid motion, swing your arms down and backward, hinge at the hips, and leap forward as far as possible, swinging your arms in the same direction.
3. Land softly and with control.

7

SPARTAN ELITE

"With your shield, or on it."

— PLUTARCH, "SAYINGS OF SPARTAN WOMEN"

A SELECT FEW OF you may want something harder after your first race. Something to push you out of your comfort zone during ordinary workouts — or the occasional legendary one.

This chapter introduces Spartan Elite Modes — methods of taking you out of your comfort zone that can be integrated into any workout. Warning: these twelve modes are inspired by ancient forms of torment and are *not* for novice athletes. This chapter also contains profiles of warriors and athletes who have truly achieved Spartan Elite status, plus Hero workouts, which embody the Spartan quality of physical and mental performance. Actually, these are less "workouts" than heroic endeavors that are rarely attempted and achieved. These endeavors may be a long-term goal or a source of inspiration, but they aren't meant for everyday training.

This chapter is for the best of the best, and those who want to become Spartan Elite.

SPARTAN ELITE MODES

HOMER (HOE-murr) — Blindfolded or in the Dark

The legendary poet Homer was blind when he composed *The Odyssey* and *The Iliad*. Perhaps that's why his memory was so good. *Practice movements while blindfolded or in the dark.* You will improve your sense of balance and relative body position (proprioception), and it will help you overcome fear or panic should you, like Jay Jackson, ever find yourself blindfolded.

TANTALUS (TAN-tuh-luss) — Fasted

Tantalus was tormented by hunger and thirst for eternity. He was forced to stand in a pool of water beneath the branches of a fruit tree, and both the fruit and water would elude his grasp whenever Tantalus reached for them — hence the word "tantalizing." *Exercise in a fasted state, and complete the workout without food or water.* Be careful about lack of water for too long, but it will prepare you for life-or-death situations when there isn't a water station or energy bar every half mile.

SISYPHUS (SISS-uh-fuss) — Unknown End

Zeus punished Sisyphus by requiring him to roll a massive boulder up a hill, then watch it roll back down again — over and over, forever. Thus, a "Sisyphean" task is never-ending. *Continue a workout until an unknown, arbitrary, or random endpoint.* Pick a landmark in the distance and keep going until you're there. Or, bring a deck of cards; after completing a minimum number of rounds, flip over a card after each round; if it's not the ace of spades, do another round; stop only when you turn over the ace of spades. Use the same method with dice and stop when you roll snake eyes. This lack of a defined endpoint will completely change your mindset.

ACHILLES (uh-KILL-eez) — Barefoot

The hero Achilles had only one weakness: his heel. Maybe he should have worked his weakness by training without shoes. *Train barefoot,* like Spartan boys did in the agoge. Start gradually — most injuries result from doing too much, too soon. Spend a couple hours per day barefoot for a few weeks before your first barefoot workout, and then increase the intensity slowly. But remember, the foot is like any other body part and grows stronger from proper use.

HERCULES (HURR-cue-leez) — Challenging Grip

The hero Hercules was known for his powerful grip. As an infant, he strangled to death two serpents that had been put in his crib to kill him; as the first of his twelve labors, he throttled the Nemean Lion with his bare hands. *Challenge your grip.* Along with your feet, your hands are the main point of contact with external obstacles — and they have to be strong. Stress your hands with uneven weights, imperfect handholds, thicker bars, rough ropes, slippery surfaces, or other methods to make everyday exercises far more challenging.

CHIMERA (kai-MEER-uh) — Mouthful of Water

The Chimera was a mythical fire-breathing creature — part lion, goat, and snake — that was slain after it choked on a lump of lead. Molten metal is a bit much, but a mouthful of water will do — like the Spartan boys who ran ten miles with a mouthful of water without spilling or swallowing it. *Complete your workout with water in your mouth.* It will force you to breathe through your nose, which is particularly helpful for athletes who compete with a mouth guard. It also turns an ordinary run into a test of mental fortitude, and you'll be amazed at how much easier your normal runs will seem.

HOPLITE (HOP-light) — Extra Weight, Worn or Carried

Hoplites marched to war carrying well over fifty pounds of armor and supplies. The most popular event in the ancient Olympics — the *hoplitodromos,* or "race of soldiers" — was a four-hundred-meter footrace while wearing a helmet, shield, and greaves (shin guards). *Wear or carry added weight during your workout.* Wear a weight vest, put a brick in your backpack, or just carry something heavy. When you exercise without the weight, you'll feel lighter and more powerful than ever.

ICARUS (ICK-uh-rus) — High Altitude

Icarus flew too high on wings of wax, which melted in the sun, then fell to his death in the sea. In other words, Icarus wasn't prepared to perform at a high altitude. Similarly, many athletes have a narrow performance window and struggle at higher altitudes. *Live at high altitude.* Unfortunately, a day or two isn't enough time for your body to adapt to high altitude. The optimal approach is to "live high, train low" — gradually adapting to lower oxygen levels at high altitude (even over years), then performing with greater intensity at low altitude.

ZEUS (ZOOS) — In the Rain

Zeus was the sky god, and storms brought down his thunderbolts. *Work out in the rain.* It's an opportunity to practice footwork, balance, stability, and grip strength. Plus, rain is a psychological barrier more than a physical one — get over it. Just don't tempt the gods by waving anything metal in the air.

POSEIDON (puh-SIGH-dun) — Cold Water

Poseidon was the sea god, wielding a trident and riding a chariot through the waves. *Get used to cold water.* Nothing invigorates like cold water. It's great for cold adaptation, reducing inflammation, and recovery. Cold showers wake you up and give you energy for the day. Try twenty seconds of cold at the end of your shower (or alternate hot and cold) and make it progressively colder and longer over time. Polar bear swims are fun too (though never do them alone). It's easy to build a cold plunge in your backyard: buy a garbage bin and fill it with cold water and ice. See how long you can last at a given temperature.

CRYO (CRY-oh) — In the Cold

The root word "cryo" comes from the Greek word for cold, as in cryotherapy or cryonics. *Exercise in the cold, or practice cold exposure.* Start by wearing one layer fewer than you'd normally be comfortable in. Be careful about appendages — especially your head, hands, and feet — but it will help you adapt to unexpected cold. If you don't shiver a little, it's probably not that cold.

THERMO (THURR-moh) — In the Heat

The root word "thermo" comes from the Greek word for hot, as in Thermopylae ("hot gates"), which was known for its hot springs. *Exercise in the heat, or practice heat exposure.* Try ten minutes in the sauna after a workout, or do some Bikram yoga (performed at 105 degrees). It's useful to train in the heat too. Be careful about dehydration and sunburn, but it will give you an edge on hot days.

SPARTAN HERO WORKOUTS

The most legendary endurance run took place in 490 B.C. — but it wasn't the marathon. The widespread legend is that the courier Pheidippides ran approximately twenty-five miles from the Battle of Marathon to Athens, announced the Greek victory over the Persians, then collapsed and died. This tale, as recounted in a nineteenth-century poem, inspired the founders of the modern Olympics to create a race called the marathon — now fixed at 26.2 miles.

But is it actually true? Storytellers exaggerate, legends grow. Which makes it all the more strange that the legend of Pheidippides has *diminished* over time.

Herodotus and the earliest Greek historians do not mention Pheidippides running 25 miles from Marathon to Athens after the battle; they recount his running 150 miles from Athens to Sparta before the battle. He arrived in Sparta to recruit reinforcements on "the day after" he left, and he didn't die on arrival. Then Pheidippides returned to Athens, presumably on foot. It was later classical historians who introduced the myth of Pheidippides' last-gasp marathon.

Until 1982, no one had thought to see if it was possible to run the 150 miles from Athens to Sparta in 36 hours, the time from daybreak to sundown the next day (in order to arrive "the day after"). So British RAF Wing Commander John Foden and four colleagues flew into Athens and plotted a course that hewed to the original description by Herodotus, which included a trip up the slopes of Mount Parthenio.

The impossible was possible: Foden ran the course in 36 hours. One step at a time.

The following year was the first official Spartathlon. And every

September since, the best endurance athletes in the world fly to Athens for the most legendary run in history: not the marathon, but the Spartathlon. Ultrarunner Dean Karnazes, whose family hails from the region, tells the story in his book *The Road to Sparta*. He sent me a picture of himself at the finish line with the statue of King Leonidas. The Spartathlon — and yes, the marathon — are the original Hero workouts.

Here are some Spartan Hero Workouts, plus some specific ideas to incorporate Spartan Elite Modes into your workouts.

AGOGE RUN

As part of their training in the agoge, Spartan boys had to run ten miles with a mouthful of water without spilling it. Start with shorter distances and develop your breathing and mental toughness, then see how far you can go. Mix it up with other modes.

- Run 10 miles #Chimera

Variations:
- Run X miles #Chimera, #Achilles (barefoot)
- Run X miles #Chimera, #Zeus (in the rain)
- Run X miles #Chimera, #Tantalus (fasted)
- Run X miles #Chimera, #Hoplite (extra weight)

BURPEE 300

Three hundred burpees is one of my favorite workouts. If you can't do 300 burpees, spread them out across a single day — then start to do them all together in a workout.

- 300 burpees for time

Variations:
- 300 burpees for time #Hoplite (extra weight)
- 300 burpees for time #Thermo (in the heat)
- 300 burpees for time #Cryo (in the cold)

SISYPHUS CARRY

Re-create the punishment of Sisyphus with an unknown number of Olympus carries.

- 10 Olympus carries, then unknown rounds of 1 Olympus carry #Sisyphus

Variations:
- 20 burpees, then unknown rounds of 10 burpees #Sisyphus
- 20 pushups, then unknown rounds of 10 pushups #Sisyphus
- 10 pull-ups, then unknown rounds of 5 pull-ups #Sisyphus

POSEIDON PLUNGE

Increase your cold tolerance by going longer at colder temperatures. Submerge your body up to the neck. Measure the temperature and keep time. Warning: Do *not* push your limits in open water; only use a cold plunge in a controlled setting with a partner. Pay attention to your fingers and toes.

- 1 minute at 50 degrees

Variations:
- 1 minute at 45 degrees
- 1 minute at 40 degrees
- 1 minute at 35 degrees

TANTALUS FAST

Warning: You wouldn't run a marathon without training, so don't jump into an extreme fast without "training" your body to function without food. Practice fasting by gradually building up the time you can go without food — sixteen hours is a good place to start. Remember, the body needs water, so don't go extended periods without water.

- No food for 48 hours

Variations:
- No food for 16 hours
- No food for 24 hours
- No food for 36 hours

BLIND BARD

You will realize how much you depend on vision only after it's gone.

- Walk across a log near the ground #Homer (blindfolded)
- Yoga or stretching #Homer
- Wrestling #Homer
- Basketball free throws, or another athletic movement #Homer
- Sandbag walking lunges #Homer

HANG TIME

This Hero workout is over once you accumulate 10 minutes of hang time on the bar. Each time you come off the bar, there is a 5-burpee penalty. Your final score is the total time it takes you to accumulate

10 minutes of hang time and complete the penalty burpees. Add a weight vest or try it blindfolded.

For time:
- 10 minutes dead hang (cumulative time on the bar)
- 5 burpees each time you come off the bar

Variations:
- #Hoplite (extra weight)
- #Homer (blindfolded) — have a partner keep time

HELEN OF SPARTA

Add Sisyphus mode for extra difficulty. Carry the sandbag on your shoulders during the runs. Race standard is a 70-lb. sandbag for men, 50-lb. sandbag for women.

For time:
- 3km sandbag run (1.9 miles) #Sisyphus (mouthful of water)
- 100 burpees
- 3km sandbag run (1.9 miles) #Sisyphus (mouthful of water)

HELL WEEK

Want huge gains but don't have much time? Here's a four-to-six-week program to get you ready for the Ultra Beast. I call it Hell Week. Experienced athletes only.

- Day 1: Run at least 60 minutes with weight (worn or carried). Bikram yoga.
- Day 2: 400m sprint, 30 burpees, 90-second rest. Repeat until you can't.

- Day 3: Lift heavy for 3–4 reps, 3 sets for each body part. Do an hour of climbing or sport.
- Day 4: Hike for 6 hours with weight in hands and on back.
- Day 5: 300 burpees, 150 pull-ups.
- Day 6: Swim for 1 hour. Bikram yoga.
- Day 7: Rest.

Given the incredible volume and intensity of these workouts, I want to share some insight from Kelly Starrett, best-selling author of *Becoming a Supple Leopard* and founder of San Francisco Cross-Fit and Mobility WOD.

Enter Kelly.

About four hundred years ago, Japan rendered up a famous samurai named Miyamoto Musashi. In addition to being considered Japan's best swordsman, he is also known for his writing and philosophy — a true warrior poet. One of his maxims is "Make your combat stance your everyday stance." On the surface, this is solid training advice: to perform with good body mechanics, practice with good body mechanics. But if we can understand the samurai's wisdom as a broader lesson, then his instruction goes far beyond footwork and fighting.

I'd like to think that Musashi wasn't simply referring to a physical stance, but our entire physical practice. Our performance in heroic moments isn't the product of a singularly heroic effort, but the result of regular actions and daily habits across our entire lifestyle. Just as a samurai's stance is the literal foundation of his performance, your regular physical practice is foundational to your performance.

When I see people decide to tackle a big physical challenge — and my wife and I are all for taking on big challenges — I witness a couple of associated phenomena. The first is that people struggle to fit in the heroic levels of training they imagine "must" be required for them to have a successful outcome. Not only is such a high-effort state transient and unsustainable, it often also leads people to neglect the rest of their lives as well as potentially causing overuse injuries. And know what happens after this? People usually return to lower levels of activity and the associated trappings of injury, weight gain, and poor lifestyle.

Does this mean we should not take on periodic, massive outputs of physical exertion? On the contrary, events like Spartan Race force us to stay focused. Goals and deadlines focus the mind on a regular physical practice that will support intermittent high-output efforts that don't "burn the house down while making toast." I wholeheartedly believe that unless you are training for some event or goal, you aren't really an athlete. You are a musician who never performs. You are an artist who never shows their work. An athlete who always practices and never performs is not a true athlete.

Therefore, if we follow Musashi's advice to make our combat stance our everyday stance, we are at once called to integrate physical practice — the Seven Pillars — into our daily lives on a sustainable basis and *actually engage in combat.* We must test body, mind, and heart to become true athletes. Our preparations are a way of life: we are heroic on a single day, and ready to be heroic every day.

SPARTAN ELITE WARRIORS

AMELIA BOONE

Amelia Boone is the winner of the 2013 Spartan World Championship. She has amassed over fifty wins and podium finishes, which makes her one of the top-ranked obstacle racers in the world. She is a full-time corporate attorney and enjoys running ultramarathons and multiday endurance events in her spare time.

It's easy to give up mentally before your body actually gives up. Handicapping yourself in training is a great way to train mental toughness, so I try to train in less than ideal conditions: midday heat, high humidity, subzero temperatures, or my favorite: the dark. Trail running early in the morning or late at night requires full engagement of your brain as well as body. Even running by headlamp is surprisingly challenging if you aren't used to it.

My favorite workouts are functional, not fancy — usually variations on "carry heavy shit over long distances." When I have access to mountains and trails, I do my own version of Olympus carry sprints. For a mountain that's seven miles to the top, I carry a heavy object — such as a sandbag or log — for the first mile and drop it. Then I sprint up to mile 2 and back down to mile 1. Then I grab the heavy object and carry it to mile 2. Then I drop it and sprint to mile 3 and back down to mile 2. Repeat all the way to the top. When living in the city, I just carried bricks up 40+ flights of stairs. And if I had a farm, there's no better workout than chopping wood for time.

COL. LIAM COLLINS

Liam Collins is a Colonel in the U.S. Army and the Director of the Defense and Strategic Studies Program at West Point. In 2007 he was the winner of the Best Ranger Competition, and now is one of the top Masters (over forty) obstacle racers in the world.

I've seen many so-called military elites who would have trouble finishing a Spartan Race. Just because someone went through a "high-speed" military training years ago doesn't mean they could do it now. Lifelong grit has more to do with your mindset than your uniform. You don't need to join the military to challenge yourself; you simply need to use your imagination or find an opportunity.

In training, I like to mix traditional workouts, such as carrying large weights over long distances, with technical events such as shooting — made tougher by environmental conditions. During one such training exercise, we had been out in the freezing rain for hours when we arrived at a station where I was instructed to give one of my soldiers an IV. My hands were shaking uncontrollably from the cold while preparing to administer the needle, and the soldier had to look away. I knew it wasn't going to get any easier after the first attempt, so I summoned the strength and focus to steady my hands just long enough to stick the needle in his vein and administer the IV — before returning to my violent shivering. I had never administered an IV to someone while shivering (almost) uncontrollably, but many times I had been cold and wet, so I had the confidence that I could do it.

You never know what obstacles will be thrown at you. You don't know when you'll have to fight your way out of a burning vehicle or cut off your leg with a pocket knife to survive. Even though you can't train these specific events, you can train your mind and body to deal with all types of adversity.

CAPTAIN A.J.

Captain A.J. is a Special Forces officer in the Singapore Armed Forces. His name has been withheld due to Singapore's Official Secrets Act.

I was a skinny, bespectacled, and awkward-looking kid. But as with all Singaporean sons who reach the age of eighteen, I was conscripted as an infantry soldier for my National Service. That's when my mindset toward life and fitness totally changed. Yes, I became physically stronger from the grueling drills, multiday field camps, live firing, and obstacle training. But I also developed a mindset that allowed me to persevere through harsh training.

To build my mental strength during my university studies — the standard route for commissioned career officers — I would deliberately choose the most boring path for my nightly march. I carried an Alice Pack with a twenty-liter jerry-can for ten kilometers or more. I tried to be as stealthy as possible in the dark of night, with no music, no training partner, and no one to cheer me on. Every night I trudged the same dreary route over and over again — with tenacity as my only source of motivation.

One of my most useful motivational tactics was to find and repeat a mantra. Some of the phrases that motivated me through those marches still echo in my mind: "Winner secure, loser pay"; "It pays to be a winner"; "Never settle for second best." Every time the training was hard or I felt like quitting, I repeated these words in my mind over and over again to tide me through. These mantras followed me every single day until they became a part of me.

In your journey to be Spartan Fit, find your own mantra to push and sustain you — until it becomes you.

CSM FRANK GRIPPE (RETIRED)

Frank Grippe is a former CENTCOM Command Sergeant Major. He served in the U.S. Army for thirty-three years, including as an infantry-man, paratrooper, and Ranger.

"One knucklehead with an AK-47 could make life interesting for us," I said to my commander and fellow Ranger. We were looking at a map of the Shah-i-Kot Valley, located in eastern Afghanistan not far from the Pakistani border, and our proposed landing zones were encircled by dominant terrain. The valley floor was at an altitude of 8,500 feet with the surrounding mountains in excess of 11,000 feet. The Soviets had attacked this valley twice in the 1980s, and both times their operations ended in disaster — hundreds of their soldiers killed or captured, and many tanks destroyed. The enemy — a mixture of Taliban and Al-Qaeda — was estimated to be one hundred or more men with varying degrees of training. There were rumors that the man himself might have escaped Tora Bora for this valley.

At 0600 on 2 March 2002 — about five months after 9/11 — I flew into the valley with an impressive group of young American warriors from the 10th Mountain Division. It was the start of Operation Anaconda — a mission to destroy Taliban and Al-Qaeda fighters — and the first significant battle since Tora Bora. Our CH-47 helicopters landed in the valley and we ran off the back ramp. I glanced back at the choppers as they lifted off, and for a fraction of a second I stood in awe of the beautiful landscape around us — until it erupted in fire from small arms, heavy machine guns, rockets, and mortars. My mountain men went right to work, taking cover and returning fire — the start of an eighteen-hour battle that would test nearly every aspect of our physical and mental fortitude.

The battle is well documented in two books — *Not a Good Day to Die* and *18 Hours* — so I will give a few examples of what happened that day and what we strive for in Spartan Race. The high altitude and cold were ever-present obstacles. Carrying a combat load at that altitude is a Herculean feat. I had a young soldier maneuver to a snowy position where he could pin down an enemy mortar team in its cave. He displayed the discipline to lie in the snow until he virtually became ineffective due to hypothermia.

The majority of our force had never experienced live combat or this intensity of enemy fire. I watched one of my young riflemen take two enemy AK rounds in the chest, which knocked him flat on his back. He got right back up and immediately returned fire. My men stopped bitching about the weight of our new body armor.

One third of our force was wounded. No one could be evacuated because of the intensity of the fight, and no reinforcements could fly in. We bandaged our own wounds. We maintained morale with humor, teamwork, and courage. The battle went on all day, and there was no way to know when it would end. And when darkness fell, we welcomed it — due to our nighttime training and equipment, we were now in charge. "We own the night" isn't just a motto.

At midnight, eighteen hours after we landed, two Army CH-47 helicopters swooped in and picked us up. Sounds simple, but that was probably the scariest part of the day since it leaves you exposed. But the enemy let us leave that night without a fight — they had enough of us. As we lifted up off the canyon floor, I stood next to the door gunner, directing him where to take aim with his machine gun. I remember looking out at Takur Ghar mountain and wondering how many of the enemy forces had survived today's fight. Even at night you could make out the blackened snow from our airstrikes.

Thirty-four hours later, U.S. special operation forces landed on top of Takur Ghar under direct fire from Al-Qaeda, fought the enemy during the Battle of Roberts Ridge, and took the mountain. And our warriors came home — with their shield, or on it.

8

THE CASE FOR THE OLYMPICS

"Citius, Altius, Fortius."
"Faster, Higher, Stronger."

— THE OLYMPIC MOTTO

THERE WILL COME a time when you've crossed the finish line of an obstacle race. Maybe two, three, or ten. I've run more races than I can count. What's next?

The first development, already well underway, is that obstacle racing will transition from a novel athletic challenge into a full-fledged sport — the ultimate human sport.

As it goes global, I'm setting a new goal for myself and my team at Spartan Race. It will be the hardest and longest endurance challenge I've ever undertaken. It won't be over in four hours, twenty-four hours, or three days. It might take me twenty years — it might take *us* twenty years. I am committed to making obstacle racing into an Olympic sport.

It won't be the first time people called me crazy. But the future of obstacle racing as an Olympic sport is bigger than Spartan Race. And too important.

Becoming an Olympic sport requires more than being popular or embodying the Olympic motto: *Faster, Higher, Stronger.* There's a long list of emerging and established sports fiercely competing for a spot that may become available should another event lose its place. The International Olympic Committee (IOC) has a detailed process for acceptance as an Olympic sport. Their criteria fall into eight categories: popularity; universality; financial viability; governance; development of the sport; care and cultivation of athletes; history and tradition; and the value that a new sport brings. Obstacle racing already fulfills many of these criteria and is laying the groundwork to fulfill the rest.

The popularity of obstacle racing is beyond dispute. It's the fastest-growing participatory sport in the world — over four million participants in more than thirty countries in 2014, eclipsing the number of people who ran 10Ks, half-marathons, and marathons, combined. Spartan Race alone accounted for over a million participants in twenty countries on four continents. TV viewers have been transfixed not only by NBC's coverage of Spartan Race, but also challenges like American Ninja Warrior and Sasuke, the popular Japanese show it was based on — which collectively air in over 157 countries. And that doesn't count the global popularity of aligned communities such as CrossFit. Obstacle racing is popular and global, exciting for participants and viewers alike.

Yet, for all its recent growth, obstacle racing isn't a fad. Throughout the past century, obstacle courses have been one of the primary methods of training and testing soldiers in militaries across the globe. Since 1944 the U.S. Military Academy at West Point has administered the Indoor Obstacle Course Test, a series of eleven obstacles designed to be the most comprehensive test of a cadet's physical fitness. The Military World Games, which hosts soldier athletes from over one hundred nations, includes obstacle racing. China's military, the largest in the world at over two million men, uses obstacle courses in basic training. YouTube videos even show Al-Qaeda recruits swinging on monkey bars, crawling through mud, and climbing over walls. Unfortunately, war is not a fad, nor are standing armies that train for war — and neither is obstacle racing.

The very origins of sport have always been closely intertwined with preparation and substitute for war. The Cherokee word for lacrosse meant "little war." And, as George Orwell wrote, "Serious sport . . . is war minus the shooting." The original events in the ancient Olympics — such as javelin, wrestling, and chariot races — were those deemed most useful in combat. Sport mimics war — and since obstacle courses are training for war, it's not hard to envision obstacle racing emerging as a sport. Other modern sports with close relations to obstacle racing include cross-country running and adventure racing, as well as the Olympic sport of steeplechase, which requires athletes to leap over barriers and water, mimicking an all-terrain dash across fields, walls, and streams.

But the origins of obstacle racing are older still. Georges Hébert was a French naval officer who helped introduce obstacle courses into the French military after World War I. His "méthode naturelle" (natural method) would give rise to parkour, whose practitioners view every bench, wall, and roof as an obstacle to overcome. Hébert was inspired by observing the strength and grace of indigenous hunter-gatherers, whose "training" consisted of the natural human movements required to survive in the wild: walk, run, jump, crawl, climb, balance, throw, lift, fight, and swim. It is how children play.

And even beyond human beings, the natural world is an awe-inspiring showcase of creatures adapted to overcome obstacles: the snow leopard's thick tail allows it to balance on a steep mountainside; the howler monkey's opposable thumbs grasp nature's monkey bars; the tiny ant carries over 1,000 times its own weight.

Messy, muddy, roughhewn nature is the original obstacle course. Navigating nature is not a fad; our distance from nature *is*. Thus, obstacle racing is not a fad so much as a return to form — a homecoming. In fact, we evolved as humans with not just the capacity, but also the necessity to run and navigate obstacles. Our nomadic hunter-gatherer ancestors survived because of this. It is our nature.

Obstacle racing is the ultimate human sport.

Therefore, it should be no surprise that obstacle racing holds universal appeal. Notably, women now make up around 40 percent of all obstacle race entrants. The top women are unquestionably elite, and the varied demands of obstacles favor a lean-and-mean body type over brute upper-body strength. And as more militaries around the globe include women, they will also participate in obstacle course training. I take a personal interest in the success of women in obstacle racing not only due to my wife and daughter, but also due to the Spartan women who were the freest and fiercest in the ancient world.

The universality of obstacle racing also extends to children. Though the majority of those signing up for the sport are aged twenty-five to forty, in line with other endurance events, the challenge of an obstacle race appeals to all ages. Most kids have to be taught how to play a sport, but all kids have an instinctive grasp of running, jumping, crawling, and climbing. Every playground is a mini obstacle course. Many sports — golf, surfing, squash, bowling — require expensive specialized equipment and playing grounds that limit access for many children. But obstacle racers need no specialized equipment or apparel, and the core components of obstacle courses are ubiquitous and cheap: dirt, wood, rope, stone, and water. It is accessible to all.

It's also not clear that any one country or region would dominate the medal podium. Obstacle racing took off in the United States, yet Kenyans have dominated the steeplechase for the past thirty years. Eastern Europeans are particularly successful in modern pentathlon, which entails the varied disciplines of horseback riding, shooting, and fencing. The Japanese excel at the challenges made famous in Sasuke, the inspiration for American Ninja Warrior. My family and I moved to Singapore to oversee the incredible growth of obstacle racing all across Asia.

Obstacle racing is for everyone, and the field is wide open.

Financially, obstacle racing makes a lot of dollars and sense. Global sponsors like Reebok and Clif Bar have made long-term commitments to the sport. The courses are inexpensive to build relative to brand-new swimming pools or high-tech stadiums. Furthermore, courses take on the character of the local geography, showcasing the most beautiful natural features of a host country. Imagine the most striking vistas of the upcoming host cities of the Summer Olympics. Rio de Janeiro's Corcovado, the local mountain topped by Christ the Redeemer, offers breathtaking views of the city below. Or, envision the national parks near Tokyo with Mount Fuji as the backdrop. World-class obstacle courses could be designed from start to finish with stunning TV shots that would not only attract viewers but also honor the natural beauty and distinctiveness of host cities. The varying terrain types and weather conditions create a uniqueness to each course. The Greek philosopher Heraclitus famously said "No man ever steps in the same river twice." So too with each obstacle course.

Furthermore, the IOC has made a priority of environmental sustainability. Obstacle racing would be an opportunity to improve the infrastructure of national parks near host cities, which are an essential but often overlooked line item in city budgets. When the Games are over, the course itself could be returned to its natural state, as opposed to a concrete-and-steel monument that quickly falls into disuse and disrepair, or it could remain an attraction to entice people into the park system. Obstacle racing is a bridge to the natural world.

The raw potential is palpable, but obstacle racing must first achieve a series of specific benchmarks for governance as a sport. This means establishing an international federation that is recognized by the IOC, overseeing at least seventy-five national federations that convene in a general assembly for at least five continuous years. The international federation would set consistent competition standards and a code of ethics, as well as set rules against doping and race fixing. Such a federation would be to obstacle racing what the International Triathlon Union (ITU) and the International Modern Pentathlon Union (UIPM) are to their disciplines — impartial overseers and advocates for the success and growth of their sports.

The International Obstacle Race Federation (IORF) was founded in 2014 to take the sport to the Olympic level. Leading the IORF is Ian Adamson, the most successful adventure racer of all time. Adamson has won seven world championships, eighteen international adventure race championship titles, and gold, silver, and bronze medals at the ESPN X Games. He won three titles on the Eco-Challenge television show, and is a three-time Guinness world record holder for endurance kayaking (262 miles in 24 hours). Not only is Adamson's race pedigree second to none, but he's also been the course and technical director for dozens of athletic events and produced television shows with partners from Mark Burnett's Eco-Challenge and Survivor. There is no figure more respected than Adamson, which makes him the perfect ambassador for obstacle racing and leader of the IORF.

The growth of obstacle race companies is a wonderful thing for the development of the sport — from fifteen promoters in 2012 to over six hundred in 2013 — even if it means more competition for Spartan Race. But the sport needs to unify around a few consistent standards to achieve Olympic caliber. Even as obstacle racing becomes more standardized, as all sports inevitably do, we are just scratching the surface of the potential obstacles in our races, and I can't wait for you to see the obstacles we're dreaming up.

At the same time, Spartan Race is in this for the long haul, and we don't cut corners that might put athletes at risk just to make a quick buck. And as a competitor and race director, Adamson understands and defends the long-term interests of athletes. Spartan Race supports the IORF's effort to establish a unified code of conduct and competition rules to meet the requirements for Olympic recognition. The first official world championship took place in Killington, Vermont, in 2014 — and we look forward to many more to come.

I couldn't be happier that some of our Spartan athletes are gaining an increasingly high profile and are starting to make a living as obstacle racers. Obstacle racing isn't about fame or endorsements, and they don't race for the money — which is exactly why I hope they ultimately get it.

As for the ties of tradition, I have to admit that building Spartan Race, rooted in the ethos of Sparta, has given me an emotional attachment to ancient Greece and a profound appreciation for the ideals embodied by the Olympics. Ancient Spartans competed in the Olympics. And the core features of obstacle racing — a multifaceted endurance run that also tests strength and athleticism — stretch back in Olympic history.

Imagine what it must have been like to attend the ancient Olympics.

The Olympic Truce meant that athletes and spectators could travel safely to the city without fear of attacks. This *ekecheiria,* the "laying down of arms," was a period when wars were suspended and local disputes put on hold — a time when real violence became symbolic violence, when aggression was channeled to nobler ends.

Citizens swarmed to Olympia, where the main stadium alone held over 45,000 spectators, with tens of thousands more in attendance. Olympia was also home to one of the seven wonders of the ancient world: a massive marble-and-gold statue of Zeus, the greatest of Greek gods. Ornate or simple, the invocation and opening ceremonies would have rivaled that of any modern Olympiad. The athletes stripped bare and competed nude to showcase the beauty of the human body — no sponsor logos, no high-tech equipment, and no pretentious apparel. The victors received nothing but a wreath of olive leaves and prestige. It was sport, pure and simple.

The roster of events started with only footraces, but eventually grew to include boxing, wrestling, pankration (a combination of wrestling and boxing), chariot racing, and pentathlon (running, long jump, javelin, discus, and wrestling). And in 520 B.C., the year of the sixty-fifth Olympiad, a new athletic event was revealed: the hoplitodromos, or "race of soldiers."

The hoplitodromos consisted of a four-hundred-meter run while clad in armor — shield, helmet, and greaves (shin guards). The wooden shield was covered in bronze, measured about three feet across, and weighed fifteen pounds or more. It wasn't just a clean sprint: Greek vases depict athletes falling to the ground and leaping over one another. It was a test of the speed, strength, stamina, balance, and agility required in battle. The event was added soon after skirmishes with the Persians, whose infamous archers had an effective range of approximately four hundred meters, which Greek hoplites had to quickly cover before engaging the enemy. The hoplitodromos wasn't a race to the finish so much as a race to the start: the frontline of battle.

The hoplite run was an immediate success. It was the last new event added to the ancient Olympics — and due to its popularity, it quickly occupied a place of honor: the final contest on the last day of every Olympic Games.

The ancient Olympics were celebrated for over a thousand years, from 776 B.C. to roughly A.D. 393, when the newly Christian Roman Empire put an end to pagan celebrations. They lay dormant for over a millennium until the visionary French educator and historian Pierre de Coubertin helped reestablish the Olympics in 1896.

At that point, the hoplite run was as much a relic as the opening prayers to Zeus. Still, Coubertin was inspired by the ancient military usefulness of the hoplite run, chariot races, and the ancient pentathlon. So Coubertin created a modern version of the pentathlon — horseback riding, fencing, pistol shooting, swimming, and running. He was also inspired by the demands of the quintessential modern soldier: deliver a message on horseback, fight a duel, shoot his way to freedom, swim a river, and run the rest of the way. Modern pentathlon was added to the Olympics in 1912 and has remained an event ever since. Obstacle racing is a thread that has woven its way from the first hoplitodromos in the sixty-fifth Olympiad through the ages up to the modern pentathlon, and it embodies Coubertin's desire for a multidisciplinary event that "tested a man's moral qualities as much as his physical resources and skills, producing thereby the ideal, complete athlete."

Tradition isn't sufficient, however — and the Olympics also considers the value brought by a new sport. Many sports are compelling in their own right — popular and exciting, financially viable, tied to tradition, sustainable, and so forth — and obstacle racing is among them. But how many new sports could add value to *existing* Olympic sports?

Obstacle racing is inherently multidisciplinary, and, as such, it serves as a point of entry into other disciplines. Steeplechase is an afterthought even to most track-and-field programs. Modern pentathlon has declined in popularity, and since it requires horseback riding and fencing, it is increasingly inaccessible to anyone but elites. But obstacle racing has already created a massive set of athletes who crave new challenges. As an example of this effect, consider how the rise of the Ultimate Fighting Championship (UFC) has reinvigorated wrestling and judo after a period of decline. Or, look at how the growth of CrossFit has increased interest in Olympic lifting and even in rowing — a sport that historically existed within the narrow banks of the Charles and the Thames. So here is the most unique value of obstacle racing: its popularity can benefit other Olympic sports.

The Olympics may span millennia, but the ideals have retained a central vision; it is the ethical code, the adherence to values such as valor, skill, striving for excellence, and pushing beyond boundaries. It's this vision that continues to make an Olympic gold medal the highest honor in sport. Not only do the Olympic Games still bring people together from all corners of the world to compete and connect regardless of their differences, but, to be part of these Games, to be called an Olympian, is to acknowledge that you believe in the stuff of legends — and the pursuit of the potential inside every human being.

It could take the rest of my years to get obstacle racing included as an Olympic sport. I have taken on a lot of insane challenges in my life. I have been told "no" more times than I can count. I have been counted out and written off. I have danced with death.

But I got it done.

And I swear an oath to every man, woman, and child who has completed an obstacle race; I swear to every young person who begins to train their talent; I swear to every Spartan warrior who died for his brothers and every Spartan woman who breathed free: I will not rest until obstacle racing is recognized as an Olympic sport.

I swear it in blood.

EPILOGUE: DOUBLE WHAMMY

AMANDA SULLIVAN WAS AN ATHLETE who loved to help others. As a girl, she used her excellence in sports to get her father out of rehab and into the bleachers. As a woman, she moved to Latin America to work with orphans, refugees, and social outcasts with Hansen's disease (leprosy). Amanda was a first responder to Hurricane Katrina, arriving in New Orleans even before the Red Cross.

In 2008 Amanda left Mexico, where she was building a shelter, and returned home to New York for Christmas. The next six weeks would change her life forever.

Amanda was about to make a right-hand turn into the parking lot of her gym. She was at a complete stop in the middle of the road, waiting for another car to exit the lot. Amanda waved for the other car to turn out, but the driver — a mother with her children — was looking at the road behind Amanda. She glanced in the rearview mirror and saw a third car, still far off but approaching quickly, and assumed it would move to the open lane to her left. Amanda waited for what seemed like forever and glanced back at the woman in annoyance. The mother's face was full of horror, and the little faces of her children were wide-eyed against the windows. Amanda looked in her rearview mirror just fast enough to see a car barreling toward her, the driver's face looking down into the glow of his phone.

The collision crumpled Amanda's car and crushed her against the steering wheel — fracturing her skull, breaking her nose and sinuses, damaging her brain, tearing the muscles in her arms, and nearly snapping her neck. The reckless driver was texting and speeding.

After leaving the hospital, Amanda spent the next five weeks at home in bed — except for regular visits back to the emergency room whenever blood and cerebrospinal fluid started leaking from her ears and nose. She started getting daily migraines (they've never stopped). But she finally reached a point where she was cleared to attend physical therapy and, hopefully, slowly regain something resembling a normally functioning body.

The physical toll of such an accident is often exceeded by the psychological trauma. But Amanda refused to give in, and when the day came for her first physical therapy session, she walked out the door with determination and positivity. She would return to Mexico to finish the shelter she started.

Amanda arrived at the medical center and parked. It was the first beautiful day in a while, and people were outside enjoying the sun. As Amanda followed a walkway toward the building, a parked car suddenly accelerated in reverse and slammed into her right side. Witnesses say she was nearly sucked under the car and they expected her to be killed, but she instinctively grabbed the top of the trunk. She was tossed upward and cracked her head against the rear windshield. People screamed and the driver slammed on the brakes, throwing Amanda off the car onto the concrete and smashing the other side of her body.

The driver, as Amanda eventually learned, was an elderly man leaving a cardiology appointment in the same building as her physical therapy. Due to his heart condition and medications, the doctor had ordered him not to get behind the wheel and instructed his wife, who was with him, to drive instead. Apparently, the man didn't even know his own name in the doctor's office. The man and his wife ignored the doctor's instructions. He later said he intended to press the brake, not the gas pedal. The elderly man passed away nine months later.

Every part of Amanda's body was broken, fractured, torn, ruptured, bloodied, or bruised. Doctors informed her that she would be permanently disabled. For three of the next four and a half years, she was confined to a hospital bed. It didn't feel like she was recovering from injuries so much as trying to survive them. Her legs atrophied from being bedridden — likely irreversible, her doctors told her, making everything worse.

There's bad luck, and then there's biblical misfortune that is so capricious and cruel that it looks like the arbitrary punishments of an angry god. To be hit by a car, not once but twice — within six weeks, the second time at the very moment she was beginning to recover from the first. And now, no prospect of full recovery.

Amanda's identity as a human being was destroyed. She had always helped others through athletics; now her body was so broken she couldn't even help herself.

"My body was deformed," she said, "and I didn't know the face that was looking back at me in the mirror. Meeting new people and having them see me as someone who was 'disabled' scared me. I started isolating myself and fell into a deep depression."

Amanda entered a dark period of anger, self-pity, and despair.

"I started questioning every decision I had made in my life that led up to my accidents. It was difficult to think clearly while being in constant pain. I felt like I couldn't really open up to anyone, because no one understood what I was going through. I felt scared."

So Amanda decided to kill herself. She bought a bottle of sleeping pills, and wrote a suicide note that furiously described every reason why she was fed up with life and lashed out at the teenager who caused her first accident, who was nowhere to be found, and the elderly man who had died. There had been no apology, no closure; her resentment was an open wound.

"This was my out," she said.

But after swallowing a few pills, she finally faced her fears.

"I realized that I didn't want to die; I just didn't want to live with this pain anymore. I didn't like being defined by things that weren't me. I was sad because I was blaming all my pain on people from whom I would never get an apology."

Amanda chose to live.

"I had to be my own hero," she said. "Life is too short to feel like a victim."

She started setting specific goals. With help from her friends at the Walter Reed Military Hospital, she constructed a "hope board," a poster covered with notes of all her near-term goals. She hung it by her bed so she could see it every day. And rather than expecting kindness from others, Amanda started to do little acts of kindness for others.

It wasn't easy, but it worked. Like exercising an atrophied muscle, Amanda's hope began to grow, and with it her confidence, strength, love, and compassion. And with her stronger motivation, she rededicated herself to physical therapy. One step after another, until the day when Amanda, using crutches, walked one mile. And then her friends convinced her to join a gym.

"And that is when everything changed. I will never be how I was before my injury," says Amanda, "but I can be better."

Amanda switched to forearm crutches and trained herself to walk even longer distances on a treadmill at the lowest speed.

And she signed up for the Tunnel to Towers 5K, which commemorates fallen firefighter Stephen Siller, who ran from the Brooklyn Battery Tunnel to the Twin Towers on 9/11. She was joined by her Wounded Warrior friends, including two triple amputees. Out of more than 30,000 participants, Amanda finished last — but she finished.

Emboldened, Amanda made more changes to hasten her recovery. She changed her diet to exclude sugar and desserts. She dropped her pain medication in favor of earning her endorphins at the gym. And she signed up for and completed a Spartan Race — even completing her burpees.

"I didn't come all the way down here to let other people do my burpees for me," she laughed. Amanda laughs a lot more these days, even about her accidents. "If you're going to get hit by a car, in front of a medical building is probably the best place."

Amanda's example has inspired others around the world. One girl with spina bifida saw a video of Amanda doing burpees on crutches, which she never realized was even possible, and became motivated to complete a Spartan Race for kids.

Amanda is a strong person, but it would be wrong to explain her turnaround by her strength or toughness. There was a shift in Amanda's mindset that took place before she cultivated those attributes. She stopped viewing herself as a passive victim and took control of her life, even if over small things. She stopped feeling entitled to an apology and proactively offered her forgiveness. She set specific goals. She accepted help from others, then helped others in return. She wasn't "kind" because she always felt that way; she *practiced* kindness. And she adopted a stoic, zen-like attitude to suffering — not running from pain, but embracing it.

"At the end of our lives, our pain is the same. What differentiates one life from another is what you do with that pain. Are you going to be angry and miserable and trapped in the darkness? Or are you going to use that pain to lift up yourself and others?"

This may be the hardest lesson of all: that pain and adversity are not just a challenge, but an opportunity—a gift from the universe, a blessing from God.

If you know what you're afraid to do, you know exactly what you should do next.

SPARTAN TRAINING PROGRAMS

This book is just the beginning. Spartan Race is constantly coming up with new ways to get people to move, to improve their mental fortitude, and to build obstacle immunity. Here are three additional ways to pursue Spartan training — for obstacle racing and all of life's obstacles. Check out Spartan.com for details.

SPARTAN SGX

Spartan SGX is the official training program of Spartan Race. We instruct top trainers in obstacle racing, and certify them to offer official Spartan Race training classes at their boxes, gyms, studios, or private practices. These classes are intended for anyone (no matter their fitness level) who wants to prepare for a Spartan Race — or just get Spartan Fit.

SPARTAN X

Spartan X is an online education course designed to develop mental toughness, resilience, and grit. This course is for any person who wants to improve their life and performance through Spartan principles, as well as any company that wants to build resilient teams and strong leaders.

SPARTAN AGOGE

The Agoge is the most extreme event in the Spartan ecosystem: a sixty-hour race that tests body, mind, and spirit. Entrance is by application only and is limited to those who have overcome major obstacles, achieved self-mastery, and embody the Spartan Code. Preference is given to endurance athletes, military, and ex-military, and those who have completed a Trifecta or Ultra Beast. It is designed for the world's toughest, most successful teams — including special sessions for U.S. military units — and is structured to be an intense, all-encompassing, life-changing proving ground. The Agoge helps participants discover the path to a fulfilling life, and achieve beyond anything they have ever done before.

FURTHER READING

ON SPARTA

Paul Cartledge, *The Spartans*

Herodotus, *The Histories*

Dean Karnazes, *The Road to Sparta*

Plutarch, *On Sparta*

Steven Pressfield, *Gates of Fire*

ON STOICISM AND OBSTACLE IMMUNITY

Mark Divine, *Unbeatable Mind*

Ryan Holiday, *The Obstacle Is the Way*

Elbert Hubbard, *A Message to Garcia*

Marcus Aurelius, *Meditations*

Seneca, *Letters from a Stoic*

Seneca, *On the Shortness of Life*

Nassim Taleb, *Antifragile*

ADDITIONAL TITLES

Joe De Sena, *Spartan Up!*

John Durant, *The Paleo Manifesto*

Christopher McDougall, *Natural Born Heroes*

Steven Pressfield, *The War of Art; The Warrior Ethos*

Kelly Starrett, *Becoming a Supple Leopard*

PRONUNCIATION KEY

Achilles *(uh-KILL-eez)*: Greek hero of the Trojan War whose fatal weakness was his heel.

Aegean *(uh-JEE-an)*: the sea between modern-day Greece and Turkey.

Agamemnon *(AGG-uh-MEM-non)*: brother of Menelaus, Greek leader in the Trojan War.

agoge *(uh-GOJ)*: intense training regimen for Spartan boys starting at age seven.

Apothetae *(uh-POTH-uhtay)*: cliff where weak Spartan infants were supposedly killed.

Chimera *(kai-MEER-uh)*: mythical fire-breathing monster, part lion, goat, and snake.

cryo- *(CRY-oh)*: root word derived from the Greek word for cold.

Dienekes *(die-ENN-uh-keys)*: Spartan soldier who died at the Battle of Thermopylae.

Gorgo *(GOR-go)*: Spartan queen and wife of King Leonidas.

gymnasium *(jim-NAY-zee-um)*: ancient Greek outdoor workout area.

Hercules *(HURR-cue-leez)*: Roman name for Greek hero Heracles, known for his strength.

Herodotus *(herr-ODD-uh-tuss)*: Greek historian, said to be the first true historian.

Homer *(HOE-murr)*: blind epic poet, author of *The Iliad* and *The Odyssey.*

hoplite *(HOP-light)*: soldiers in the Spartan military.

hoplitodromos *(HOP-lit-oh-DROME-ohs)*: ancient Olympic foot-race in full armor.

Icarus *(ICK-uh-rus)*: mythical figure who died after his wings of wax melted in the sun.

Iliad (ILL-ee-add): Homer's epic poem about the Trojan War.

Lacedaemonia *(LASS-uh-day-MOHN-ee-uh)*: the region of Greece ruled by Sparta.

Leonidas *(lee-oh-NAI-dus)*: Spartan king who died at the Battle of Thermopylae.

Lycurgus *(lie-CURR-gus)*: legendary Spartan king and lawgiver.

Marcus Aurelius *(MAR-kus ow-RAY-lee-us, uh-RAY-lee-us)*: Roman emperor and Stoic.

Menelaus *(MEN-uh-LAY-us)*: Spartan king during the Trojan War, Helen's husband.

Odysseus *(oh-DISS-ee-uss)*: legendary Greek hero and protagonist of Homer's *Odyssey.*

Olympus *(uh-LIM-puss)*: the highest mountain in Greece and home of the Greek gods.

Panhellenic *(PAN-hell-LEN-ic)*: related to the whole of ancient Greece.

Pericles *(PERR-ih-kleez)*: Athenian statesman, orator, and general during its Golden Age.

perioikoi *(PER-ee-OY-koy)*: free noncitizens who lived in the region under Spartan rule.

phalanx *(FAY-langks)*: rectangular mass military formation of heavy infantry.

Pheidippides *(fie-DIP-uh-deez)*: courier whose epic running inspired the modern marathon.

Poseidon *(puh-SIGH-dun)*: Greek god of the sea.

Seneca *(SENN-uh-kuh)*: Roman Stoic philosopher, statesman, and playwright.

Sisyphus *(SISS-uh-fuss)*: legendary Greek king doomed to push a rock up a hill forever.

Sophocles *(SOFF-oh-kleez)*: ancient Greek playwright known for his tragedies.

Spartiate *(SPAR-tee-eight)*: a male Spartan citizen, also known as a "peer."

Tantalus *(TAN-tuh-luss)*: Greek mythical figure punished with eternal hunger and thirst.

Taygetus *(TIE-gay-tuss)*: a mountain near Sparta, legendary location of the Apothetae.

thermo- *(THURR-moh)*: root word derived from the Greek word for hot.

Thermopylae *(thur-MOP-uh-lee)*: "hot gates," location of the famous battle against the Persians.

Thucydides *(thoo-SID-uh-deez)*: Athenian historian and author of *The Peloponnesian War.*

Xenophon *(ZEE-nuh-fon)*: Greek historian, soldier, and student of Socrates.

Zeus *(ZOOS)*: Greek god of sky and thunder, and king of the gods.

SPARTAN RECIPES

Real food is simple food; cooking doesn't have to be complicated. According to Plutarch, the Spartiates ate the same simple fare in the messes every day — though we don't expect most readers will start making their staple dish, black broth: pig's blood, salt, and vinegar. Black broth aside, we've tried to adhere to a Spartan ethos with the included recipes. Unlike many cookbooks that include needlessly complicated meals for rare occasions, we've focused on simple staples that don't require a lot of effort and that taste great — plus a few of my favorites, such as baked garlic bulbs and fermented beet juice. Spartan up and give them a try too!

Breakfast
- Barn Beast Breakfast Burritos
- Broccoli Egg Muffins
- Buckwheat Chia Pancakes
- Paleo Banana Waffles
- Warrior Porridge (Aztec Edition)

Lunch
- Avocado Egg Salad
- Blueberry Turkey Burgers
- Quinoa Salad with Avocado Dressing

Dinner
- Baked Salmon with Fresh Herbs
- Grilled BBQ Shrimp Kebabs
- Spartan Rice and Beans
- Spinach and Lentils with Quinoa Noodles

Veggies, Roots, and Tubers
- Spartan Baked Garlic Bulbs
- Spartan Roasted Asparagus
- Ginger Sweet Potato Mash
- Spartan Baked Beets
- Roasted Butternut Squash

Snacks
- Banana Almond Muffins
- Kale Chips
- Sweet Potato Chips
- Spartan Guacamole
- Mango Avocado Salsa

Desserts
- Almond Cocoa Apple Trail Cake
- Banana Coconut Rice Pudding
- Cantaloupe Popsicles
- Chocolate Avocado Pudding

Smoothies and Beverages
- Beet Kvass
- Blueberry Banana Chia Smoothie
- Kale Lemonade

BREAKFAST

BARN BEAST BREAKFAST BURRITOS

15 minutes | 4 servings (2 if you're the Barn Beast) | vegetarian, gluten-free

During a one-hundred-mile snowshoe race, the infamous Barn Beast, aka Jason Jaksetic, requested breakfast burritos. Here is the burrito recipe to commemorate the historic event.

Ingredients:

6 eggs	4 corn tortillas
½ cup Greek yogurt	1–2 tbsp. olive oil
½ cup chopped tomato	sea salt
½ cup chopped green pepper	fresh black pepper
½ cup chopped onion	¼ tsp. red pepper flakes (optional)
½ cup cooked black beans	

Directions:

1. In a bowl whisk the eggs, Greek yogurt, salt, pepper, and red pepper flakes.
2. In a medium skillet coated with olive oil, sauté vegetables and beans until soft.
3. Pour the egg/yogurt mixture over vegetables and cook until mixture sets.
4. Once firm, divide egg mixture among the warmed tortillas. Roll each into a burrito. Garnish with salsa.

Recipe courtesy of Jason Jaksetic, Spartan lifestyle editor

BROCCOLI EGG MUFFINS

30 minutes | 6 servings | paleo, vegetarian, dairy-free, gluten-free

Eggs and broccoli pair well together — enjoy them in your omelets, burritos, and, yes, muffins. Wrap them up for an egg burrito, adding your favorite salsas. These muffins are easily stored and transported in plastic bags or containers (though refrigerate until used). Go nuts with this recipe, adding in all your favorite veggies.

Ingredients:

6   eggs
1   broccoli crown
1   jalapeño pepper

3-5   mushrooms
1-2   tbsp. olive or coconut oil

Directions:

1. Whisk eggs in bowl.
2. Chop up vegetables.
3. Oil bottom of muffin tray (olive or coconut oil works well).
4. Pour eggs into muffin tray — only halfway. They'll expand, and you want room for veggies.
5. Drop in vegetables. Don't overfill muffin tins.
6. Bake at 350°F for 15–20 minutes.

Recipe courtesy of Jason Jaksetic, Spartan lifestyle editor

BUCKWHEAT CHIA PANCAKES

20 minutes | 2 servings | vegetarian, gluten-free, dairy-free

These pancakes are pure power and energy while being deliciously satisfying. When you combine buckwheat and chia in pancakes you are doubling down on the protein when compared with traditional pancakes.

Ingredients:

1 tsp. coconut oil for cooking

1 cup buckwheat flour

1 egg

2 tbsp. chia seeds

2 tbsp. cacao powder

2 tbsp. cacao chips

2 tbsp. maple sugar (optional)

1 tsp. baking powder

1 cup almond milk

Directions:

1. Oil up skillet or pan with coconut oil.
2. Mix all ingredients in bowl.
3. Pour pancake-size amount of batter on skillet/pan.
4. Flip pancakes (usually they are ready right after any small bubbles form and pop).
5. Serve with a little honey or maple syrup.

Recipe courtesy of Jason Jaksetic, Spartan lifestyle editor

PALEO BANANA WAFFLES

30 minutes | 4 servings | paleo, vegetarian, gluten-free, dairy-free

Fuel up with this paleo-inspired take on breakfast. Waffle irons got their start in the ninth and tenth centuries with the creation of communion wafer irons. Now we're giving waffles an update with this grain-free, dairy-free recipe. Works as pancakes too.

Ingredients:

2 ripe bananas

1 tbsp. coconut oil

1 tbsp. cane sugar (optional)

1 pinch sea salt

1 pinch ground nutmeg

3 eggs

¼ cup coconut flour

¾ cup brown rice or almond flour (or other non-gluten flour)

1½ cups coconut milk

1 tsp. baking powder (aluminum-free)

Directions:

1. Peel the bananas and mash them well in a bowl.
2. Add the rest of the ingredients one by one, mixing everything together thoroughly.
3. Heat up the waffle maker and cook the waffles one at a time.
4. Serve with a little maple syrup and fresh fruit.

Recipe courtesy of Rose-Marie Jarry, chef and athlete at Kronobar.com

WARRIOR PORRIDGE (AZTEC EDITION)

20 minutes | 1 serving | gluten-free, vegan, dairy-free

Chia and quinoa are two superfoods from Central and South America. Chia is about 14 percent protein by weight and 40 percent fiber — and is easy to mix with most staple meals. Quinoa is notable among plants for containing all essential amino acids. Double down on awesome with this superfood porridge.

Ingredients:

- ¼ cup quinoa (dry)
- 2 tbsp. chia seeds
- 1 tbsp. maple syrup
- dash of cinnamon
- dash of sea salt
- fruit, berries (optional)
- coconut milk (optional)

Directions:

1. Cook quinoa in 2 parts water (½ cup) to 1 part quinoa. Bring to boil first, add quinoa, and then lower to simmer, covered, for 10–15 minutes or until liquid is absorbed.
2. Add chia seeds, maple syrup, cinnamon, and sea salt. Stir everything together.
3. Add fruit and/or coconut milk, if you have some. Relish in your hearty Spartan warrior breakfast.

Recipe courtesy of Andrew Thomas

LUNCH

AVOCADO EGG SALAD

30 minutes | 1 serving | vegetarian, gluten-free

This egg salad might look a little green, but it's all good. The Greek yogurt gives it a consistency that is somewhere between sour cream and mayo. Also delicious to wrap in lettuce.

Ingredients:

4 eggs

1 avocado

4 tbsp. Greek yogurt

4 big romaine lettuce leaves (optional for lettuce wraps)

Directions:

1. Submerge eggs in a pot of cool water. Slowly bring water to boil, then cover the pot, turn off the burner, and let sit for 10–12 minutes. Run under cold water and peel.
2. Dice eggs and avocado.
3. Mix eggs and avocado with the Greek yogurt.
4. Serve on lettuce leaves, crackers, or salad.

Recipe courtesy of Jason Jaksetic, Spartan lifestyle editor

BLUEBERRY TURKEY BURGERS

30 minutes | 4–5 servings

Take people by surprise at your BBQ by putting some fresh-picked summer blueberries into their burgers. The toppings suggested below are mostly for keeping with our red, white, and blue theme, but do anything you please with your blueberry turkey burgers.

Ingredients:

1 lb. ground turkey
2 garlic cloves, minced
4¼ cups flour
½ cup blueberries (fresh or frozen)

1 egg
Toppings: white cheddar or Swiss cheese, tomato, mayo, ketchup

Sourdough hamburger buns

Directions:

1. Combine turkey, garlic, flour, blueberries, and egg in a bowl and mix with your hands.
2. Mold the mixture into 4 or 5 patties.
3. Cook patties on a grill, flipping occasionally.
4. Add toppings and serve on sourdough buns, if desired.

Recipe courtesy of Jason Jaksetic, Spartan lifestyle editor

QUINOA SALAD WITH AVOCADO DRESSING

20 minutes | 2–4 servings | vegetarian, gluten-free

This quinoa salad will be your go-to gluten-free and vegetarian lunch. It stores great and doesn't even need to be reheated to be delicious. Make up a big batch on Sunday night and then eat it as a ready-made lunch the next few days. Just store the dressing in a separate container. Substitute any vegetables you're craving.

Ingredients:

1 cup quinoa (raw or sprouted)

1 can corn (or other vegetable), drained

1 can black beans, drained

½ avocado, peeled

½ cup plain yogurt

1 tbsp. lemon or lime juice

1 tsp. soy sauce (gluten-free)

1 tbsp. olive oil

Directions:

1. Bring 2 cups water to a boil.
2. Add quinoa, then reduce heat to a simmer. Cover and cook for 15 minutes.
3. Remove from heat and let sit for 5 minutes.
4. Heat corn and beans.
5. Combine dressing ingredients in a blender and blend till smooth.
6. Serve quinoa on plate and cover with corn and beans. Add dressing on top or the side.

Recipe courtesy of Laura Nally

DINNER

BAKED SALMON WITH FRESH HERBS

30 minutes | 2 servings | paleo, pescatarian, dairy-free, gluten-free

Baking salmon couldn't be easier, and fresh herbs are your ticket to intense flavor. Once you start to cook with tinfoil in the oven, you'll never go back.

Ingredients:

14 oz. fresh wild salmon (2 small filets)

2 tbsp. coconut oil

2 tbsp. chives, chopped

2 tbsp. parsley, chopped

2 tbsp. basil leaves

2 tbsp. lemon thyme

2 garlic cloves

pink Himalayan salt and ground pepper

Directions:

1. Place each filet onto a foil sheet.
2. Split all the remaining ingredients in half, place them on each fish filet, and close the foil.
3. Bake in the oven for 20 minutes at 350°F.

Recipe courtesy of Rose-Marie Jarry, chef and athlete at Kronobar.com

GRILLED BBQ SHRIMP KEBABS

15 minutes | 4 servings | paleo, pescatarian, gluten-free

Put another shrimp on the barbie! Grilled shrimp is delicious and easy, but it's less common than burgers and dogs, so you'll look like a master chef.

Ingredients:

½ lb. raw deveined shrimp

1 green pepper

1 medium red onion

barbecue sauce
(check ingredients for
dietary restrictions)

skewers (wooden or metal)

Directions:

1. Wash vegetables. Cut into 1-inch pieces.
2. If using wooden skewers, soak them in water 30 minutes in advance. If using metal skewers, spray or brush with oil.
3. Preheat grill to medium-high.
4. Thread shrimp and vegetables alternately onto skewers.
5. Grill kebabs for 4–7 minutes, brushing often with barbecue sauce.

Recipe courtesy of Jason Jaksetic, Spartan lifestyle editor

SPARTAN RICE AND BEANS

1 hour cook time, plus 8+ hours soak time | 4 servings | vegan, gluten-free

This staple is great to make in bulk, refrigerate, then add to meals throughout the week. These instructions are for raw beans, but canned beans and instant rice are convenient alternatives.

Ingredients:

1 cup black turtle beans (raw)

1 cup brown rice

Directions:

Beans Prep:

1. Remove any funky-looking beans or non-bean debris.
2. Wash beans in a colander.
3. Soak beans overnight in refrigerator.
4. Rinse beans thoroughly in colander.
5. Boil beans in water for 1 hour. Add water if needed.
6. Test beans with a fork to see if they are ready.

Rice Prep:

1. Bring 2½ cups of water to boil, then add rice.
2. Reduce heat, cover, and simmer until tender, 20–30 minutes.
3. Let stand 5 minutes, then fluff with a fork or spoon.

Mix:

1. Heat rice and beans together in a saucepan.
2. Serve with your favorite salsa, Greek yogurt, or cheese.

Recipe courtesy of Jason Jaksetic, Spartan lifestyle editor

SPINACH AND LENTILS WITH QUINOA NOODLES

30 minutes | 4 servings | vegan, gluten-free

Quinoa creates a nutritionally dense pasta that is higher in protein than traditional flours and is also gluten-free. Paired with the nutrient-rich spinach and lentils, it's a savory and filling dish.

Ingredients:

1   box quinoa noodles

6   tbsp. coconut oil

4¼ cups soy sauce
    (gluten-free)

6   garlic cloves, diced

2   cups cooked lentils

3   cups spinach, chopped

    salt and pepper

Directions:

1. Boil water and cook the noodles per instructions on box. Strain and set aside.
2. In a pot, melt the coconut oil. Add soy sauce and garlic. Sautée for 1 minute.
3. Add the strained noodles, lentils, and chopped spinach. Cook for 1–2 minutes.
4. Add salt and pepper to taste.

Recipe courtesy of Rose-Marie Jarry, chef and athlete at Kronobar.com

VEGGIES, ROOTS, AND TUBERS

SPARTAN BAKED GARLIC BULBS

25 minutes | 2 servings | paleo, vegan, gluten-free

Baked garlic bulbs give you garlic paste, which is a versatile part of your cooking arsenal. You can put it in hummus or use it as a spread on bread, vegetables, or meats.

Ingredients:

2   bulbs of garlic
2   tbsp. olive oil

Directions:

1. Preheat oven to 400°F.
2. Cut the top ¼ inch off the garlic bulbs, exposing the tops of the garlic cloves inside.
3. Pour a bit of olive oil over each bulb and then place them in an oven-safe dish.
4. Bake garlic for 35–45 minutes, or until light browning can be seen on exposed garlic bulbs.
5. Let cool.
6. Using your fingers, squeeze the individual garlic cloves out from the bulb.
7. Mash into a paste if desired.

Recipe courtesy of Andrew Thomas

SPARTAN ROASTED ASPARAGUS

15 minutes | 4 servings | paleo, vegan, gluten-free

Once you start roasting vegetables in the oven, you'll never stop. Use tinfoil to minimize cleanup. Genius.

Ingredients:

1 lb. asparagus spears

2 tbsp. olive oil

2 tbsp. minced garlic

salt and pepper

Directions:

1. Preheat oven to 425°F.
2. Snap off the very bottom of the asparagus.
3. Mix olive oil and garlic in a baking dish or bowl.
4. Rub asparagus with half of the olive oil and garlic.
5. Roast in oven for 10–20 minutes.
6. Once asparagus is cooked to desired crispness, pour remaining olive oil and garlic over asparagus, add salt and pepper, and serve.

Recipe courtesy of Jason Jaksetic, Spartan lifestyle editor

GINGER SWEET POTATO MASH

30 minutes | 4 servings | vegetarian, gluten-free

Pass on your regular mashed taters and try this delicious alternative when dishing out your favorite entrees. Simple and sweet.

Ingredients:

2	large sweet potatoes	1	tbsp. butter
1½	tbsp. fresh ginger, diced		salt and pepper
1	tbsp. brown sugar or maple syrup		

Directions:

1. Boil sweet potatoes in salted water until tender, then drain well.
2. Mash sweet potatoes with ginger, brown sugar or maple syrup, and butter.
3. Add salt and pepper to taste.

Recipe courtesy of Jason Jaksetic, Spartan lifestyle editor

SPARTAN BAKED BEETS

50 minutes | 2 servings | vegan, gluten-free

If you're looking for an easy and tasty way to incorporate beets into your diet, try baking them. Baked beets are a rich source of phytonutrients called betalains, which possess strong anti-inflammatory and detoxification effects.

Ingredients:

4 medium beets   drizzle of olive oil
   pinch of sea salt

Directions:

1. Preheat oven to 400°F.
2. Rinse beets and wrap each beet in tinfoil.
3. Bake for 45 minutes, checking for tenderness with knife.
4. Remove from oven with oven mitts, unwrap tinfoil, and rinse under cold water.
5. Pull/peel skin off beets under running water (should come off pretty easily).
6. Cut beets into quarters or slices, add a drizzle of olive oil and a pinch of salt, and serve.

Recipe courtesy of Andrew Thomas

ROASTED BUTTERNUT SQUASH

1 hour | 2–4 servings | paleo, vegan, gluten-free

Eating baked squash is like eating a baked potato. No one will fault you for eating the skin — it's edible, contains nutrients, and has a unique texture. Otherwise just eat the soft flesh by using your fork, much like you would a sliced-open baked potato. Use squash puree as a fresh alternative to canned pumpkin.

Ingredients:

- 1 butternut squash
- 2 tbsp. coconut oil

salt and pepper

a few dashes of cinnamon (optional)

Directions:

1. Preheat oven to 350°F.
2. Wash squash.
3. Cut squash in half lengthwise, then cut across to make quarters.
4. Use a spoon to scrape out the pulpy insides and seeds into a bowl. (You can eat these seeds raw or roast them.)
5. Place squash in baking tray.
6. Use your fingers to rub the exposed flesh with coconut oil. The coconut oil is going to lock in the flavor as the squash cooks, so go for it. Rub in some cinnamon, if desired.
7. Bake flesh-side up for 45–60 minutes at 350°F. The more it cooks, the bolder the flavor gets. Serve warm, adding salt and pepper to taste.

Recipe courtesy of Jason Jaksetic, Spartan lifestyle editor

SNACKS

BANANA ALMOND MUFFINS

30 minutes | 6 servings | paleo, vegetarian, gluten-free

When you start baking your own treats, you'll marvel at how you can eliminate loads of sugar without compromising flavor — like with these muffins.

Ingredients:

3   bananas
½   cup almond butter
½   cup sliced almonds
1   egg
1   tsp. vanilla extract
¼   cup cane sugar (optional)

1½   cups almond flour or quinoa flour
1   tsp. baking powder
½   tsp. baking soda
½   tsp. salt

Directions:

1. Grease a muffin pan or use muffin wrappers.
2. Preheat oven to 350°F.
3. Mash bananas.
4. Mix the almond butter, almonds, egg, vanilla, and sugar together. Give it a good stir.
5. Add flour, baking powder, baking soda, and salt. Mix again. Stir well.
6. Pour mixture into muffin pan.
7. Bake for 18–20 minutes.

Recipe courtesy of Jason Jaksetic, Spartan lifestyle editor

KALE CHIPS

30 minutes | 2 servings | paleo, vegan, gluten-free

Don't expect to be able to do any heavy salsa lifting with these. But what these kale chips lack in sturdiness they make up for in flavor and nutrition.

Ingredients:

3–4 kale leaves
2–4 tbsp. olive oil

salt and pepper
red pepper flakes (optional)

Directions:

1. Preheat oven to 425°F.
2. Cut out center stem of each leaf.
3. Toss kale in bowl with 1–2 tablespoons olive oil and the spices. One teaspoon of each spice is a good place to start, unless you are craving some extra salt or spice — then add more.
4. Pour 1–2 tablespoons of olive oil in baking sheet.
5. Place kale pieces in one layer on baking sheet.
6. Bake for 20 minutes, or until crisp.

Recipe courtesy of Jason Jaksetic, Spartan lifestyle editor

SWEET POTATO CHIPS

45 minutes | 3–4 servings | paleo, vegan, gluten-free

Sweet potato chips are an art form. Slice them too thick and they won't be crisp; too thin, and they'll burn up around the edges. Be warned: you'll have to keep an eye on them for the first few times till you've mastered your stove.

Ingredients:

2 thin sweet potatoes

1–2 tbsp. coconut oil

salt and pepper

red pepper flakes (optional)

Directions:

1. Wash potatoes.
2. Slice potatoes. Try to make them between a quarter and silver dollar in thickness.
3. Lay on baking sheet. (Parchment paper is always a good idea.)
4. Brush or rub melted coconut oil across top of chips.
5. Season.
6. Bake at 400°F for 30–45 minutes. At the 20-minute mark flip chips on sheet and move them around so they don't stick.

Recipe courtesy of Jason Jaksetic, Spartan lifestyle editor

SPARTAN GUACAMOLE

5 minutes | 4 servings | paleo, vegan, gluten-free

This guacamole is truly spartan in its ingredients. Avocados are packed with good fats and other beneficial nutrients, including vitamin K, fiber, folate, and potassium — but feel free to add your favorite fruits and vegetables into the mix (tomato, red onion, cilantro, jalapeño peppers, or mango). Makes a smooth and tasty sandwich spread. Leave an avocado pit in your bowl of guacamole to help preserve it longer.

Ingredients:

4 avocados
1 small lime

1 tsp. sea salt

Directions:

1. Cut avocados in half, remove pits.
2. Scoop avocados out from peel and into a bowl.
3. Cut lime in half and squeeze juice from both halves into the bowl of avocados.
4. Add salt. Mash and mix well.

Recipe courtesy of Jason Jaksetic, Spartan lifestyle editor

MANGO AVOCADO SALSA

15 minutes | 8–10 servings | paleo, vegan, gluten-free

Salsa is another Spartan staple — good with sweet potato chips, eggs, and wraps. If mangoes aren't available, just drop them for a more traditional salsa. Remember, how finely you dice your ingredients will greatly affect your salsa-dipping experience. Slack off on the chopping, and your chips will break beneath the massive bulk of your salsa.

Ingredients:

3 tomatoes, diced

1 green pepper, diced

1 lime, juiced

2 cloves garlic, minced

1 mango, diced

1 avocado, diced

½ cup minced fresh cilantro

dash of salt

Directions:

1. Dice all ingredients.
2. Mix all ingredients together in a bowl.
3. Serve with chips, or on chicken, fish, or pork.

Recipe courtesy of Laura Nally

DESSERTS

ALMOND COCOA APPLE TRAIL CAKE

45 minutes | 8–12 servings | vegetarian, gluten-free

Skip all the fancy energy bars with additives and preservatives, and hit the trails with your own freshly baked power supply.

Ingredients:

1 cup almond butter

1 cup unsweetened applesauce or honey

3 eggs

¼ cup cane sugar (optional)

1 tsp. vanilla extract

½ cup buckwheat flour

1 tsp. baking powder

⅓ cup cocoa or cacao powder

Directions:

1. Mix all ingredients together.
2. Bake for 40 minutes in 9 × 9 pan at 300°F.

Recipe courtesy of Jason Jaksetic, Spartan lifestyle editor

BANANA COCONUT RICE PUDDING

1 hour | 4–6 servings | vegan, gluten-free

Asia has been doing desserts like this for a long time. This tropical take on your after-dinner snack will have you rethinking the possibilities of pudding.

Ingredients:

4 cups almond milk

1 cup Arborio rice

1 can coconut milk

1 banana, mashed

½ cup shredded coconut

dash of cinnamon

Directions:

1. Mix almond milk and rice in a saucepan.
2. Bring to a boil, then reduce heat and let simmer for 30 minutes, stirring occasionally, or until rice is tender and floating in a creamy sauce.
3. Stir in the coconut milk and mashed banana, and let simmer an additional 10 minutes. Stir well.
4. Let cool.
5. Toast the coconut in a pan on medium heat for 4 minutes, or until light brown.
6. Serve the pudding in bowls, garnished with the toasted coconut and cinnamon. Serve warm or chilled.

Recipe courtesy of Jason Jaksetic, Spartan lifestyle editor

CANTALOUPE POPSICLES

3 hours | 6–8 servings | vegetarian, gluten-free

Popsicles aren't hard to make, so skip the freezer section. Have the kids help out on this one.

Ingredients:

1 cantaloupe
½ cup Greek yogurt

2 tbsp. honey

Directions:

1. Slice the cantaloupe in half, remove the seeds, scoop out the flesh, and put in a blender.
2. Add remaining ingredients to blender and blend.
3. Pour puree into Popsicle molds and freeze. No molds? Try an ice-cube tray with toothpicks.

Recipe courtesy of Jason Jaksetic, Spartan lifestyle editor

CHOCOLATE AVOCADO PUDDING

30 minutes | 4 servings | paleo, vegan, gluten-free

One bite of this creamy dessert and you will marvel at how delicious whole foods can be.

Ingredients:

3 dates

2 ripe avocados

2 tbsp. coconut oil

⅓ cup maple syrup

½ cup cocoa powder

1 tsp. vanilla extract

¾ cup almond milk

Directions:

1. Soak the dates in warm water for 15 minutes.
2. Add coconut oil, dates, syrup, vanilla, half of the almond milk, avocados, and cocoa powder into a blender.
3. Blend until smooth. Add additional almond milk until the pudding is the consistency you want.
4. Spoon into bowls, cover, and chill.
5. Serve with your favorite fruits and nuts as toppings.

Recipe courtesy of Jason Jaksetic, Spartan lifestyle editor

SMOOTHIES AND BEVERAGES

BEET KVASS

5 minutes (prep time) | 6–8 servings | paleo, vegan, fermented, gluten-free

This traditional Eastern European fermented beet beverage is a great example of how food can be a powerful medicine. Beet kvass is loaded with healthy probiotic bacteria that are essential for a strong immune system and good digestion. If this is your first experience with a homemade ferment, be prepared for some new and interesting flavors. Seven days of fermentation is pretty intense — first timers, go for three days. If the taste is too overwhelming, all is not lost: serve over rice and eat the vegetables.

Ingredients:

3 medium-sized beets
4¼ cups small green or red cabbage

2 tbsp. salt
filtered water

Directions:

1. Peel and chop beets into 1-inch cubes.
2. Chop up cabbage.
3. Place cabbage into a large glass jar (½ gallon is ideal), followed by the beets.
4. Add salt to the jar.
5. Fill jar with filtered water to 1 inch from the top of the jar.
6. Seal jar and store at room temperature for 3–7 days.
7. Strain out the beets and cabbage, and store liquid in refrigerator to drink.

Recipe courtesy of Andrew Thomas

BLUEBERRY BANANA CHIA SMOOTHIE

5 minutes | 1 serving | paleo, vegan, gluten-free

Smoothies are an easy breakfast on the go or after workouts: peel, blend, and drink. Using a frozen banana adds a cool and refreshing quality to your smoothie, plus frozen bananas last until you use them. (Tip: peel bananas before freezing them.) Frozen blueberries are great too, since you can buy in bulk and eat them year-round. Chia seeds absorb water like crazy — up to 12 times their own weight — so coconut or almond milk delivers a smoother drink. And avoid letting a chia smoothie sit too long or it might resemble a pudding.

Ingredients:

1 banana	2 tbsp. chia seeds
½ cup blueberries	1 cup unsweetened coconut milk

Directions:

1. Put ingredients in blender.
2. Liquefy ingredients.

Recipe courtesy of Jason Jaksetic, Spartan lifestyle editor

KALE LEMONADE

5 minutes | 1 serving | paleo, vegan, gluten-free

If you don't really dig vegetables, juicing them is a great way to incorporate them into your diet. Kale lemonade is simple if you have a juicer.

Ingredients:

3	large kale leaves	2	lemons
1	apple, cored and chopped	1	cup filtered water

Directions:

1. Wash kale, apple, and lemons.
2. Remove thick center rib of kale leaves and core apple.
3. Process all ingredients in juicer.

Recipe courtesy of Jason Jaksetic, Spartan lifestyle editor

ACKNOWLEDGMENTS

A book is an endurance race of a million obstacles, large and small. I couldn't have finished this one without the help of a team of dedicated contributors.

First, I want to thank my coauthor, John Durant. He picked up this 200-lb. sandbag of a project, put it on his shoulders, and ran uphill. I never had to explain to him why Spartan is so much more than a race. From ancient Sparta to modern times, I'm grateful for his help articulating the Spartan lifestyle, mindset, and movement. You're one of us — AROO!

David M. DeLuca was like that invaluable utility player on the team who rose to the occasion and came up big in the playoffs. Research, editing, drafting sections, creative thinking — David did it all, and he did it with a smile, at all hours of the day and night (including weekends). He improved every part of the book. I also want to thank Jeff O'Connell for his incredible help on this project, an extension of our successful collaboration on *Spartan Up!*

My agent, Marc Gerald at the Agency Group, was always there to steer us true. We were happy to work with Susan Canavan, my editor, on our second project together. She has a talent for channeling our Spartan energy and enthusiasm into a clean and focused manuscript. Many thanks to the entire team at Houghton Mifflin

Harcourt, who do so much work behind the scenes to perfect the final product.

I'm blessed with an awesome team at Spartan that eagerly helped on a book project even when it wasn't in their job description. Joe DiStefano, our director of training, not only helped design the workout program, but also helped us push the envelope with Spartan Elite modes. Jason Jaksetic not only lent the story of his personal pilgrimage, but also helped put together the Spartan Recipes. Marion Abrams, who runs the Spartan Up! Podcast, helped us corral material from our interviews. Thanks to Grant Reitz for design work on icons for the book, and Katlyn Evans for tracking down action photos. Daniel Goldstein (Skywalker) produced new exercise photos, courtesy of photographer Rory Doyle and athletes Jody Lupien and Brandon Welti. The Spartan recipes include delicious contributions from Rose-Marie Jarry, Andrew Thomas, Laura Nally, and Carrie Adams. Siobhan Colgan helped on the manuscript during a key period. Many thanks to members of the Spartan team who helped behind the scenes: John Gauch, Kenneth Koleyni, and Darren Braham. The entire staff at Spartan Race helps make it all possible. And I'd also like to acknowledge the good people at Reebok for being great partners who help us fulfill our mission.

So many incredible people contribute to the Spartan universe. I'm grateful to Jay Jackson and Amanda Sullivan for sharing their survival stories — you exemplify the Spartan ethos every single day; thank you for inspiring others to do the same. Steven Pressfield was gracious and generous with his time — thank you for bringing Sparta to life. Ian Adamson continues to work tirelessly for obstacle racing to become an Olympic sport — he's a true champion, and we're grateful for his efforts. And I have to thank some of the extraordinary athletes, soldiers, and leaders who contributed to the book: Dean Karnazes, Dan Edwardes, Zach Even-Esh, Amelia Boone, Col. Liam Collins, Captain A.J. (you know who you are),

CSM Frank Grippe (Ret.), and Kelly Starrett. Thank you to Jeffrey Zurofsky and Frank Bisci, PhD, for their help on guiding the nutritional recommendations. You're all-stars and loyal friends.

A special thanks to those who helped me find different ways to discover and rediscover fitness over the past forty years. My mom, for introducing me to good food, yoga, meditation, and monks. I don't know where I'd be without Bikram yoga. Uncle Pat showed me a long, long bike ride as a young teenager. Thanks to Chet Warman for a much longer bike ride. Yan and Chad from Reebok, for another way. Dr. Bisci, for how to eat. Cousin Anthony, for handing me the book *Raw*.

And, of course, family is everything. Thank you to my parents, Ralph De Sena and Jean De Palma. I'd like to think I inherited grit and stubborn perseverance from my father and a lifelong love of health from my mother — a good combination for an endurance athlete and entrepreneur. Many thanks to my sister, aunts and uncles, cousins, and good friends for your love and support.

To my children, Jack, Charlie, Catherine, and Alexandra: I'm so proud of each one of you.

To my wonderful wife, Courtney De Sena: Did you have any idea what a crazy adventure our life would become? I think you did — and yet you still joined me on it, which is why I love you so much. You *are* the linchpin.

Finally, to every man, woman, and child who has run a Spartan Race and embodies the Spartan Code: AROO!